SUCCESSFUL REAL ESTATE INVESTING

CLIFF HOCKLEY

CPM, CCIM, MBA

SUCCESSFUL REAL ESTATE INVESTING

INVEST WISELY, AVOID COSTLY MISTAKES AND MAKE MONEY

NEW YORK

LONDON • NASHVILLE • MELBOURNE • VANCOUVER

SUCCESSFUL REAL ESTATE INVESTING
INVEST WISELY, AVOID COSTLY MISTAKES AND MAKE MONEY

© 2019 Cliff Hockley, CPM

Published in New York, New York, by Morgan James Publishing. Morgan James is a trademark of Morgan James, LLC. www.MorganJamesPublishing.com

ISBN 9781642793208 paperback
ISBN 9781642791570 eBook
Library of Congress Control Number: 218907422

Cover & Interior Design by:
Christopher Kirk
www.GFSstudio.com

Morgan James is a proud partner of Habitat for Humanity Peninsula and Greater Williamsburg. Partners in building since 2006.

Get involved today! Visit
MorganJamesPublishing.com/giving-back

INTRODUCTION AND ACKNOWLEDGMENTS

When I graduated from Willamette University with an MBA in 1981, I never expected to work as a property manager or commercial real estate advisor. But one thing led to another, and in 1986 I joined my in-laws in their business. My goal was to run a company, and my father-in-law, mother-in-law, brother-in-law, and wife allowed me to grow within the framework of S. Bluestone Realty. We had fewer than ten employees at the time, but today there are over eighty great people who work with me at Bluestone & Hockley Real Estate Services and SVN Bluestone & Hockley.

The purpose of this book is to help teach both the novice and the experienced real estate investor how to make money and avoid mistakes that I have encountered over the years as a property manager and real estate investor. This book gives concrete examples of good and bad decision making when it comes to investing, giving the reader an opportunity to learn from those successes and failures. Investing in real estate has enabled me to become successful and accrue millions of dollars in real estate assets.

Investing in real estate is often portrayed as an easy way to get rich, but that does not work for every investor or with every investment. Real estate investing involves many variables: location, cash flow, upside, opportunity, quality of products, financing, good management, the economy, and last but not least, your emotions.

This book is designed to help you learn through various short stories, or "tales." These tales describe common decisions that real estate investors make—and not all of them are good decisions. Use these stories as a road map to chart your future real estate success.

Finally, this book would not have been possible without the support of my wife, Julie and our children, Ellen and Lily and my parents. Additionally, the following people were instrumental in getting this book to press: Heather Hill, Annie Leung, Ali Shaw, Dehlia McCobb, Allie Ross, Shannon Mattin, and Vanessa Van Eaton.

I was also fortunate to have and greatly appreciate the help from the following: Diane Danielson, COO of SVN International; Joe DeCarlo, Principal at JD Property Management Inc.; Joe Weston, Managing Member of Weston Investment Company, LLC; Doug Marshall, President of Marshall Commercial Funding; Paul Challancin; Ralph and Carolyn Hockley; and Pat Coan—all of whom took the time to read this book and make valuable comments and additions. Any factual errors are my own, and I take full responsibility—enjoy.

TABLE OF CONTENTS

PART I:

DREAMS

1 THE GET RICH QUICK MYTH

Name: Mitch
Property Type: Mobile Home/Land
Famous Last Words: "I've finally figured out how to get rich quick!"

The advertisement screamed from the TV: "Invest $39.99 for an introductory kit that will teach you all the tricks to buying real estate." The well-known pitchman claimed he was involved because he believed all Americans should share the American dream.

Mitch leaned over and picked up the phone. At thirty years old, he was still living with his parents, bouncing from one low-paying job to another, and all he really wanted was a get-rich-quick solution to jumpstart his life. The ad said he could buy the program with no money down—perfect! It promised that he would make money from every real estate transaction and become a millionaire, even without investing any of his own cash. As Mitch dialed, he vaguely heard the salesman mention that the program focused on foreclosures, but he never stopped to think about why this might or might not be a good idea.

The Easy Purchase

Mitch charged the $39.99 on his credit card, and one week later he received ten CDs and a textbook that provided a step-by-step approach to buying foreclosed real estate.

As directed by the kit, Mitch planned to start making phone calls and visit sheriff's sales in his county. At his very first auction, he listened as the announcer described a quarter-acre of land in his county with a three-bedroom home on it. The bidding started at $50,000, and to Mitch's surprise, no one else spoke up. *What's wrong with them?* he thought. This was clearly a perfect property at a fantastic price. He vaguely remembered the textbook advising he sit through one whole auction before ever bidding on anything, but this was just too good to pass up.

Mitch eagerly raised his auction paddle. "I'll take it!"

The auctioneer asked if anyone else wanted to bid against Mitch, and the room was eerily silent. Mitch didn't care—he was on track to get rich quick. When the auction was finished, Mitch was directed to a cashier's line and handed a stack of paperwork. He'd expected that somewhat, but what he didn't expect was the top form demanding 20 percent down within twenty- four hours. Hadn't the program promised he wouldn't have to spend any of his own money? Mitch was puzzled, but when he started to ask the cashier about it, she said firmly, "No exceptions," and informed him that he'd have thirty days after paying the deposit to arrange financing to close the deal.

There was no turning back now.

Mitch quickly borrowed money from his parents to get a $10,000 cashier's check ready. They seemed hesitant to hand over the money, but Mitch knew they also wanted him to move on with his life, and this seemed to be the only way. Even though the kit had promised no money down, Mitch didn't see a problem with paying a $10,000 down payment. And since it was borrowed money, it was essentially none of his own money down.

The Hard Reality

After paying the deposit, Mitch ran out of the sheriff 's office with a broad smile on his face; he was on his way to being rich. He jumped into his car and drove out to look at the property. The sheriff's office had given him the legal description of the property at the auction, so he figured he would have no trouble finding it.

But five hours later, he was still driving around lost, so he called the sheriff's office for directions. He finally found the property in a desolate part of the county on a gravel road. There was no sewer service, and water came from a well. The nearest neighboring home was ten miles away.

This property was in the middle of nowhere—good for growing marijuana and not much else. When Mitch opened the door and it fell off its hinges in his hand; he realized the sheriff had probably seized the home in a drug raid. The property had been ransacked. Doors and windows were broken; there were no appliances. Mitch was crushed.

Two Choices

At this point, Mitch had three choices: either give the property back or try to fix it up and then sell it or rent it.

Without much thought, he raced back to the sheriff's office and begged, "Please give me back my $10,000. That property is a dump." The sheriff's clerk responded by pulling out the sales contract and pointing out that the deposit was nonrefundable.

Flashes of the next fifteen years played in Mitch's mind. With a failed property investment, he'd not only have to keep living at his parents' house, but he'd also have to work twice the hours at his endless string of low-paying jobs just to pay them back for the deposit. And keeping the property was not an option. He didn't want to live there, he didn't want to find financing for the other $40,000 he owed on the property, and he had no money to invest in fixing it up to make it livable, rentable, or sellable. He felt hopeless.

A man hanging out by the door of the sheriff's office said, "I'll give you $4,000 for your interest in the property." Mitch recognized him as one of the other bidders at the auction and negotiated him up to $5,000, finally ridding himself the property for what was at least not a total loss.

Mitch had to work an extra job for a year in order to pay the other $5,000 back to his parents. In a way, Mitch was lucky. He was able to get out before he got badly hurt or spent more money. He threw away the get-rich-quick kit.

Starting Over

After a while, despite his bad experience, Mitch realized that real estate investment was not necessarily a bad idea—he just needed to go about it in a smarter way. He started reading books and magazines on real estate investing whenever he had a free moment. He always made sure they were written by people experienced in investing and not just making promises that were too good to be true.

Mitch also started attending foreclosure auctions just to see how other investors decided what to buy and how to go about it. He learned that investing well in auction properties required being at the right place at the right time and having the experience and financing pre- arranged to get. a good deal. It is always helpful to have cash available. Most successful dealmakers say no to a hundred deals before they find the right one. He also learned that no one successfully buys a property without seeing it first. Good investors look up the auction information in advance and visit properties they're interested in.

Even after they pay the deposit, they're not locked into buying yet—they schedule inspections of the boundaries, zoning, environmental codes, lead-based paint, and plumbing and electrical first. They also obtain estimates of how much repairs and upgrades will cost, and they work that into their budgets.

With time, Mitch did successfully buy a property from an auction—two, actually. He fixed the first one up and sold it, making enough of a profit to buy himself a nice home and move out of his parents' house.

Lessons _____

1. You're not going to get rich quick buying real estate. It takes research, time, and planning.

2. Never trust a "no money down" gimmick. Even with financing options, real estate generally takes at least a little bit of cash.

3. Always see a property before you buy—no exceptions. Get it inspected too.

2 THE ART OF BECOMING A REAL ESTATE MOGUL

Investor Profile

Name: Leon
Property Type: Houses/Shopping Mall
Famous Last Words: "All you have to do is rent it out. The rest of it takes care of itself."

L eon had wanted to invest in real estate since he was ten years old. In his future, he saw himself as another Donald Trump, owning large office buildings and casinos and living a life of opulence. From a young age, he'd been telling all his friends that he was saving to buy real estate. Now was the time to do it.

A Wannabe Real Estate Mogul Is Born

Leon was twenty-one when he closed on his first investment house in Galveston, Texas. This house was in a dingy area of town, but he had saved all the money for the down payment and closing costs. He rented the property to the first tenants who showed interest, and it made a little money, $100 a month.

He immediately put that profit aside to save for his next house, and within four years he purchased his second investment property. In the meantime, he earned a reasonable wage as an appliance salesperson. Ever conscious about his image, he upgraded his car every chance he got until he finally drove a black Mercedes CLS 550 with leather upholstery to try to impress his friends with his success as a landlord. He never wanted to drive his nice car through the dingy neighborhood he owned property in though, so he put the houses out of sight, out of mind, assuming everything was fine with them.

Troubles Start Brewing

Before long, Leon encountered trouble with his first tenants, not surprisingly since he hadn't screened them. One of the tenants was busted by the police for growing marijuana in the house. Leon had received earlier warnings from the police, but he needed the cash flow from the rent, so he had chosen to ignore them. Now that the issue had escalated, the police were threatening to seize the house because he had not acted on their warnings. He narrowly escaped losing his property by producing a forged eviction letter. Thank goodness the police didn't catch on to the forgery, or he could have lost the house and so much more.

In the other house, Leon had rented to a single mom. When he received a call from her that there were roaches, he promptly called the exterminator, who reported back to him that the house was filthy, and the roaches would continue to live there until she cleaned up. Leon sent her written notices and even inspected the property—nervously, as his Mercedes sat vulnerable out front—but he could not get her to improve her level of cleanliness. Finally, he asked her to move.

His next tenant in this house was also challenging. She was in her sixties, and according to her application, should have been a model tenant. But she moved in her son, an ex-convict, and his friends started showing up. Leon explained to her that her son was not on the rental agreement and therefore not an approved tenant, but she adamantly refused to throw him out. The police sent additional notices to Leon and notified him that the son was a convicted sex offender. The son and his friends made the neighbors nervous, and pressure from the neighbors eventually convinced Leon to ask the tenant to leave. She threatened to sue for age, race, and religious discrimination, so Leon, at his wit's end with her, agreed to pay her $5,000 to motivate her to move. Leon figured he was just having a run of bad luck.

Try, Try Again

Leon did not let these problems deter him from his dreams. He was a good salesperson and had been promoted to sales manager at the appliance store. Soon he made enough money to start planning his next investment. After all those tenant headaches, Leon sold the two houses and bought a small commercial strip shopping center instead. He felt pretty good about the deal. There were three tenants: a national coffee chain, a cell phone store, and a small convenience store with a couple of gasoline pumps. Leon also picked a better location this time. He left the dingy residential area behind and was now a property owner in the Strand Historic District in the Galveston marina. Thinking he was smart for planning ahead, he bought extra flood and hurricane insurance.

His commercial property seemed to be operating better than his two houses had, at least until the national coffee chain closed five hundred stores, including the one in his property. Thankfully he had a good lease and was able to collect a two-year rent buy out from the tenant, which bought him time to find another tenant. He found a local coffee roaster to take the place of the national chain, but he had to take a 20 percent reduction in the rent. By then, he was just happy he had a tenant. Then, when the cell phone store gave him notice that it would not be renewing its lease, Leon wondered if the gods were conspiring against him.

As Leon was pondering how he was going to fill the vacancy, Hurricane Ike blew into Galveston and destroying most of the town and 50 percent of his building. He had insurance to cover the damage, but the building was without power and water, and no one knew how long it would take to rebuild Galveston.

Moving On, Eventually

After all that, Leon realized the bad luck wasn't just in renting to residential tenants or in living in a hurricane-prone area. His bad luck had come because he had been in such a hurry to get rich that he hadn't taken the time to research, screen, and plan well.

When his building was finally repaired, and his tenants were back in business, Leon decided that rather than use the profits to immediately upgrade his car or buy the latest tech gadgets, he would put the money in savings to be available to cover the unexpected—who knew when another hurricane would blast through or another national chain would go under, leaving him without rental income for months on end?

And most importantly, Leon finally accepted that he didn't know everything. He interviewed attorneys so that he would have a good one on hand in case he ever had legal problems with a tenant again. Leon even got back into residential properties, but this time he joined a rental housing organization and became familiar with the local landlord/tenant laws. He also learned how to screen for better tenants in advance to help prevent problems before they even came up.

Leon did one thing right from the beginning, though—he always kept his insurance up to date. Only now, he had learned that it takes more than insurance to plan ahead and anticipate that things could go wrong at any time. Before long, he was making enough of a profit to take care of both the expected and the unexpected and started looking for his next investment.

Lessons _____

1. Be humble. You can learn a lot easier by asking questions and researching than by making mistakes and paying for them.

2. Have good professionals on hand so you can ask for help when you need it.

3. Expect the unexpected.

3 DREAMS, BIG MISTAKES

Investor Profile

Name: Jake
Property Type: Apartments
Famous Last Words: "Why start small when you can jump straight to the big moneymaking properties?"

Jake envied the way his friends were investing in real estate. He had big dreams and wanted to trump all his friends. They were buying 20,000-square-foot neighborhood shopping centers and fifty-unit apartment buildings. He was going to be smarter and buy bigger.

The Wrong Zone

Jake had an edge on the average investor because his father had given him $5 million to invest on his twenty-fifth birthday. He purchased a beautiful piece of land located in the path of growth on the edge of Portland, Oregon. It was just big enough to handle the 100-unit apartment property he wanted to build.

He had not checked into the zoning and learned too late that he had spent $1 million on a piece of land that was zoned for farming only. Sure, it was in the path of growth, but it was not designated to be added into the urban growth area for another hundred years. He was fortunate to be able to sell it to a farmer and make back his $1 million.

That mistake got Jake's attention. He was not only embarrassed for having bought too quickly, but he also could have lost money.

His father agreed. "Twenty percent of your stake was a lot of money," he warned. "But you'll do better next time."

Jake sensed that his father wanted to give him advice, but he was intent on doing it all himself. He'd never seen his father ask anyone for help, after all, and Jake wanted to prove that he was just as capable of a real estate investor and business owner as his father was.

The Right Zone Is Not Enough

Jake tried again, but this time he had a lawyer review the zoning and give him tips regarding construction laws for apartments before closing on the land purchase. He bought the suburban property for cash, out of pocket with plenty of money set aside for construction.

Then he decided to build. He was twenty-six and thought he knew everything, so he planned the complex to appeal to young people, the kind of hip twentysomethings he figured would like to live together as roommates. He planned for 40 four-bedroom, four-bath units; 20 two-bedroom, two-bath units; 20 one-bedroom, one-bath units; and 20 studios. He put in a huge clubhouse with a party room, big-screen TV, kitchen, pool, ping-pong table, weight room, tanning bed, and sauna. With all those amenities, he thought he could charge a $20 monthly fee per person to use the clubhouse. He also added an apartment manager's office to the clubhouse, and he planned for one hundred allocated parking spaces for the property.

He wanted beautiful landscaping, so he hired a local landscaper to install a meditation garden and create a motif of Japanese plants. Finally, he got the permits to build. The architects had done a wonderful job of designing the property. Jake had estimated the construction costs at $90 per foot, so it was close to competitive in the marketplace.

"It's beautiful," Jake's father told him as they toured the nearly completed construction site. "Have you thought about—"

"Trust me, Dad, I've thought of everything." Jake held his hand up to his father. "You'll see."

It took one year to build the complex, and on May 1, it was ready to open for residents—except Jake had not even thought about residents. He had no management company, no on-site manager, and no maintenance staff.

Had he gone through a bank to finance the purchase and construction, an advisor would have asked him the tough questions about every last detail. Or had he listened to his father, he might have thought of these details. Jake was dumbfounded when he discovered that there was more to owning a property than just building it.

"That's all right, son," his father comforted. "Just do what you can now to fix your mistakes." Again, Jake's father started to offer him advice, this time on selecting a good property management company and anticipating tenant needs.

But again, Jake stopped him. "I got it, Dad."

So, Jake interviewed three management companies and promptly hired one. The property manager was very successful for the first fifty units but then ran into a problem. The property only had one hundred parking spaces, and the way Jake had designed the apartments, they needed 250 spaces. If the property had been downtown, it might have been sufficient, but in the suburbs, everyone needed a car to go to school or work.

In addition, Jake had not built a room for a maintenance office or storage for repair parts. Jake was flummoxed. He had significant capital tied up in the property, and it was only half leased with rents barely at market value.

His father suggested he buy additional land to create more parking spaces, and as much as Jake didn't want advice, he knew this was a good idea. He bought a lot next to his apartment complex, but it took a year for Jake to convince the city that he should be allowed to use it for parking. Finally, they reached an agreement but only after making 25 percent of the property into a city park. He also had to submit paperwork to the city, so he could add on to the clubhouse to make room for the maintenance department and supplies.

By now, Jake was twenty-nine and tired. He'd spent four years making mistakes, one after another.

His father tried to calm him down over a coffee. *"Mistakes are part of the process. We learn from them and move on."* He shrugged, but then his tone got a little more serious. *"Sometimes you can learn what you need to know before the mistakes are made, though."*

Jake figured he knew where his father was going with this, but he decided not to interrupt this time.

"You have a lot of resources at your disposal—and I don't just mean me. There are professional advisors you can hire, and there are plenty of good books you can read to make sure you don't overlook important details." Jake started to realize that the more he learned, the more there was to learn.

Smaller and Safer

Jake now realized that he should've started with a smaller project. Then he could've made the same mistakes and not squandered his inheritance.

Once the apartment complex was full, Jake found a job with an apartment developer in town, where he learned many lessons he should have known before he started purchasing and developing property.

When he started his next project, a ten-unit infill property, he asked his father if he had any input.

His father smiled. *"You've used your resources well."* Now Jake knew he was on the right track.

Lessons _____

1. Make your mistakes on smaller projects before you step up to bigger ones.

2. There's always something you haven't thought of. Talk to knowledgeable people or read up on issues you haven't worked with before, so you can avoid mistakes as much as possible.

PART II:

MAKE THE PURCHASE

4 THE IMPORTANCE OF GOAL SETTING

Investor Profile

Names: Trudi and Claus
Property Type: Retail Buildings
Famous Last Words: *"Retirement will just happen. It's not something you need to plan for."*

Helene learned about Trudi and Claus when she inherited them as clients from her mentor. She saw that they'd moved from Bavaria to America in their mid-twenties, bought a few buildings in Lancaster County in Pennsylvania, and built a great business by making wurst, salami, and other German meat products in the Pennsylvania Dutch country, where everyone spoke German. It had been twenty years since they had bought property, and when Helene called to see if they were interested in meeting with her about new properties, they politely declined. Two weeks later, though, they called her back. Her call had gotten them thinking, and they were now considering selling their business and retiring. Claus. in particular, was tired of the wurst business.

When the three of them sat down together to discuss their exit plan, Helene started by asking, "How much money do you have saved for retirement?"

Trudi looked at Claus, and Claus stared blankly at Trudi. "Do we have enough money to retire?" Trudi asked him.

"I thought you were paying attention to our investments," Claus responded.

"I thought you were," Trudi said.

Helene learned that Trudi and Claus had split up the responsibilities for their real estate investments—Trudi was the property manager and kept the books, and Claus was the buyer of the properties. However, they never really discussed what their goal was. They had a loose plan to buy real estate, but they didn't know if they were making money or not.

Claus had purchased the building where their store was located, and then he purchased the buildings around the store in case he wanted to grow the business. Their other properties were retail locations that sold their wurst. But Trudi and Claus had never tallied their asset values, depreciation shelter, or rental income and expenses. They lived in the same house but had never talked to each other about these matters.

Planning

Before Trudi and Claus got too angry with each other, Helene waved her hands between the couple. "It's all right. We'll just have to evaluate all those details now and set up a plan. Although it's easier if you do all that in the beginning and every year along the way, it's not too late to look at the details, set goals, and plan for your retirement."

Once Helene had the details of the existing investments straight and confirmed that the couple had some money but not enough to retire, she brought up the subject of goals with Trudi and Claus. She started by discussing two levels of goal setting for the real estate investor: micro and macro.

"At the micro level," she explained, "the investor sets goals for each individual real estate investment regarding budgets and returns. Each property should have a set of goals." She went on to list what those goals should focus on:

- How long to hold (when to exit)

- What kind of a loan to get (terms, rate, etc.)
- How much leverage the investors are comfortable with
- How much money to spend on capital improvements
- How strong the on-site and off-site management is
- When to review monthly financials and cash flow of each asset
- When to set aside time to pay attention to real estate holdings

Trudi and Claus nodded, so Helene went on. "At the macro level, the investor sets goals regarding the performance of the whole real estate portfolio."

Her examples included:

- How big the portfolio should be
- How much real estate needs to be in place to help fund retirement
- The vision for how to reach the asset and return goals
- How long it will take to reach those goals
- How to assemble the cash to achieve those goals

She explained that these goals should be reviewed in an annual planning session with each other or the investment partners to ensure the investments are performing the way everyone wants. And Helene advised them to consider tax planning during this process, accounting for the following taxes:

- Standard federal, state, and local income and sales taxes
- Short-term capital gains
- Long-term capital gains
- Depreciation recapture
- Alternative Minimum Tax

Risks

Then Helene covered risks. Astonishingly, Trudi and Claus hadn't faced many setbacks in their twenty years of business, but they weren't closing up shop quite yet. This was important information for them to know.

Clearly there are always risks in real estate investment. Common questions include: Can we insure ourselves for the downside? How do we recover?

Are all our eggs in one basket? Trudi and Claus already knew this in general, but Helene pointed out three specific major risks: weather, economy, and overleveraging.

For weather, Helene warned: "You can insure for many weather-related risks, including earthquakes, tornadoes, hurricanes, and floods, but be sure to read your insurance policies carefully and realize that the insurance companies will not cover everything. Not all policies are the same, either. All policies have deductibles, and you'll want to always make sure you have the cash to cover deductibles."

Then she brought up risks related to the economy and its effect on tenants. "What happens if you buy a multifamily property in a market like Houston or Oklahoma City, where there's limited land-use planning and the cost of land and construction is inexpensive?" Trudi and Claus didn't know, so Helene told them, "In those markets, apartment vacancies can run from 10 to 20 percent. Does your investment model tolerate such vacancy rates? Every marketplace is different due to the local economy, land use, and planning regulations. Real estate investors need to watch closely to understand their specific marketplace."

Helene concluded with questions about overleveraging. "I see that you've been making high monthly payments on your mortgages. I'm sure that's because you have a great income and can handle negative cash flow and you wanted to accelerate your reduction on the principal balance. But what happens if you can no longer work? Is there enough money available in cash flow, or would you need to sell your investments to generate cash? Whenever you consider selling, too, it's important to ask if the time is right to sell or refinance your investments. Are market trends and interest rates in your favor?"

With all Helene's questions, Trudi and Claus could see that they weren't going to retire right away, but with a plan and Helene's help, they could do it in the foreseeable future.

Enacting the Plan

Because of this discussion, Helene helped Trudi and Claus diversify their investments. They sold two of their retail centers and bought a single-tenant investment property and an apartment property instead. They then agreed to meet once a month to review their financial documents and the returns on their properties. They also charged their business a little more rent and planned to sell some of the other buildings, so they wouldn't be as tied to their business for retirement income. This was a breakthrough that helped them see that they could reach their retirement goals—just in time.

Lessons _____

1. Talk to your investment partner about the details, no matter how much you trust each other. Something could always slip through that neither of you are paying attention to.

2. Setting goals for each property is as important as actually buying property.

5 SURPRISE NEW PROPERTY

Investor Profile

Name: Maureen
Property Type: House
Famous Last Words: "I inherited a house? What will I do with that?"

Maureen was twenty-five when she started learning about investing in real estate. She had just started her first job and was barely making ends meet. Student loans were killing her, and she was unable to pay for her work wardrobe, the commute, and the rent. Then she inherited a home that had belonged to her favorite Uncle Rudy. At first, she wasn't sure what to do with it. It was located in a small town a two-hour drive from her apartment and job, so it wasn't a convenient place for her to live, and the idea of selling it to pay off her debts was very appealing. She then consulted her dad.

"Do you think Uncle Rudy would have minded if I sold his house to pay off my debts?" Maureen asked her dad over the phone.

"Not at all, sweetie," he said. "Are you sure that's what you want to do, though? You could have an extra stream of income by renting it out." Maureen hadn't even thought about that option. She listened while her

25

dad explained that she could use the money from the rent to help her pay her bills. When she said she was worried that the distance was too far for her to manage the property, her dad offered to come pick her up the next weekend and they could inspect the house together.

Envisioning Possibilities

That weekend came swiftly, and Maureen was glad to see her dad. The idea of deciding what to do with this house alone was overwhelming—what if she made a money-losing decision? She didn't want to let her uncle or her dad down, but she also knew she didn't have a lot of time or money to be a property manager.

"Just keep an open mind, honey," her dad advised.

The house was a cute three-bedroom, two-bath Cape Cod home with a view of a lake. As they walked through the empty house, Maureen's happy memories came flooding back—the days of spending the lazy hot summers running around the yard, jumping into the lake to cool off.

The house was in pretty good condition. Uncle Rudy had remodeled before his death, and the old wallpaper had been removed. New light fixtures and carpeting had been installed, and the kitchen had received a facelift.

Maureen's father spoke first. "You own this free and clear. The estate taxes have been paid off. It's worth about $150,000, and I think it's in good shape. I think it would rent for $1,500 a month."

Maureen pondered that for a second and asked, "Does that mean I would clear $1,500 a month?"

He shook his head. "No, I don't think so. You'll still have property taxes to pay, plus insurance, utility bills, turning costs between tenants, and maintenance expenses. And because you live so far away, you'll probably want to hire a property manager. I think you might clear $800 a month."

Maureen turned to look out the picture window, thinking a small family would be comfortable in this home.

Her father continued, "The benefits of owning the home as a rental are significant. First of all, the property is going to appreciate. Second, the tenants will be helping you pay down your other debts, and you'll have immediate positive cash flow."

Maureen nodded. "Yeah, those are some pretty compelling reasons to keep the house rather than sell it."

"This is a huge opportunity for you." Her dad placed a comforting hand on her shoulder and looked out the picture window with her. "This could be your first step to financial independence."

Finer Details

"All right." Maureen turned toward him. "Let's do it. Let's go find some tenants."

Her dad chuckled. "Hold on, not so fast. First you need to set investment goals now that you're a real estate investor." He told her that the first goal to set was to estimate the income she expected her investments to generate, now and in the future.

"The $800 you mentioned sounds good to me," she said, wondering why it needed to be so complicated.

"Excellent, but it's also good to set an annual goal of real estate values and equity you want to reach."

They wandered out to the patio and sat on the porch swing while Maureen learned that to reach these goals, she could take various paths:

- After holding this property for a time and letting its value appreciate, she could sell it and, using the IRS permitted 1031 tax deferred exchange, she could buy another, more valuable property. "Maybe a duplex or a fourplex," her dad said. This way she could increase her cash return, appreciation, and depreciation, which could even shelter her rental income from taxation.

- She also had the option of refinancing this house after a few years and using the equity she earned to buy another property.

- "Or," her dad said, "as you make more money, you could save some of it to buy other homes or investment real estate."

"That's so much to think about!" Maureen cried.

Her dad laughed. "I know, but any of these options would allow you to grow your net worth and, over a period of time, buy your financial freedom.

And no matter what path you take, Uncle Rudy would be okay with it. He loved you. Just consider your options and do what's best for you."

"Okay, I want to keep the house and then decide on refinancing, selling, or other options later."

She stood up. "For now, let's go find a local property manager to get it rented and keep an eye on it for me. Then I need you to help me plan my real estate investing future."

Her dad stood up too. "You bet. I'll even show you how to retire at fifty like I did."

"Nah, I want to retire at forty-five!" she half joked.

They laughed together and went into town to find a property manager.

Lessons _____

1. Just because you're not right in town or have other debts doesn't mean you can't own a rental property. It can be a good setup.

2. There are four ways to make money investing in real estate: cash flow, appreciation, depreciation, and debt reduction.

3. Set short-term and long-term plans for your property, like how much you want to earn, how much you want your real estate to be worth, and when you might want to refinance or sell to buy more real estate.

6 BEWARE OF UNDERLYING LOANS

Investor Profile

Name: Rita
Property Type: Industrial Park
Famous Last Words: "All loans are basically the same. Just sign the paperwork and pay them off as soon as possible."

Rita was excited about the opportunity she had. Her mother had agreed to invest with her in a 40,000-square-foot industrial park that they were buying for $4 million. What's more, her mom was giving her full control of the purchase and management, basically acting as a silent business partner. To Rita, this meant her real estate–savvy mother trusted her. She felt proud, capable, and eager.

The Enticing Loan

The six-building industrial park was a classic incubator business park design, located on 3.4 usable acres with twenty-one tenant spaces. Each warehouse space included an overhead roll-up door and 100 square feet of office space. It was designed to be functional for a broad range of light industrial uses. The ceiling heights were fifteen feet, and the siding was a T-111 wood product with masonry trim. The submarket vacancy rate was just 2.5 percent, though this property was only 86 percent occupied with seventeen tenants. The location had a lot of on-site parking and was close to a major freeway and a major commercial artery.

Rita used a conduit, also known as commercial mortgage-backed securities (CMBS) loan at 5.25 percent over a twenty-five-year term, which made this deal appealing in a market when interest rates were in the 6.5 percent range for new mortgages. These loans typically have low interest rates, established terms and solid prepayment penalties designed to have you hold on to the loan until its term expires. This is because the loan to split into tranches and sold to many owners to reduce risk, which makes the loan difficult to assume, or sell early, because the investors are promised a fixed yield.

When Rita was eighteen, her mom had made some investments for her and at the same time suggested she work for a property management company to learn the ins and outs of the real estate business. With this experience, she thought she was very real estate savvy and did not hesitate to put down $1.5 million plus costs to obtain the loan, which locked her into a yield maintenance prepayment penalty for the first ten years of the loan. Rita and her mom had always held real estate over the long term, so she didn't really worry about the terms.

Dancing in the Streets

The day the deal closed, Rita was thrilled. Champagne poured freely, and tears of happiness were flowing down her cheeks. This was her first deal, and she had done all the due diligence—had gone through multiple inspections, had verified zoning, and had reviewed all the leases very carefully— so she felt she was buying a property with lots of potential. She sealed and striped the parking lot, painted the buildings in new funky colors, modernized the awnings, and changed the signage to update the park.

Occupancy

Once Rita was done updating the property, she focused on increasing its occupancy rate. First, she negotiated lease extensions with all the tenants in the property, and then she aggressively marketed the space with the help of a well-established commercial real estate broker. She tried many different approaches to entice new tenants, including free rents and major tenant improvement concessions, but she was only able to attract one more tenant to the property, bringing the occupancy rate to 90 percent. Several times, she came close to renting out the last 10 percent, but something would always happen, or another tenant would move out, leaving Rita's property perpetually 90 percent occupied.

Finally, she decided she should refinance in order to improve the structure of the deal. That way, she could still make a reasonable profit even at just 90 percent rented. However, when she called the bank to discuss refinancing, she was told she couldn't refinance without paying off the prepayment penalty.

The Sale

After two years of struggling with the property, the shine had worn off, and Rita decided to sell it. Her rents had increased, and at a 90 percent occupancy rate, she was able to command a small increase in value to $4.3 million, just enough to cover closing costs and commissions.

She listed her property, and the broker asked her about the underlying loan. She explained that there was a conduit loan with a large prepayment penalty that would expire in eight years. "No problem," he said.

Five months later, though, there were no offers on Rita's property because no buyer wanted to put up $1.8 million for the down payment. The prepayment penalty was calculated at about $400,000, so she couldn't reduce her sale price. Rita didn't want to disappoint her mom and take a loss, though. She was at her wit's end.

This investment had only cost money rather than making money. The rent was barely covering her mortgage and the cost of property upkeep. She had worked her way through $200,000 in cash reserves, and even with all of her experience in managing property, she was not breaking even.

She changed real estate brokers. The new broker finally found a buyer to take the property but not without significant concessions on her part.

At her broker's suggestion, she took a loss on the deal to move it, but it still took five months to arrange the assumption of the existing debt and finally close the deal. Rita was disappointed and angry with herself, and she was embarrassed that she had lost a portion of her mother's money.

On the other hand, she decided not to do another conduit deal with a yield maintenance prepayment penalty, and she had learned to first read the financial fine print before she borrowed money, for her future investments.

Lessons _____

1. Read the fine print for every loan.

2. Make sure you have some cushion between the payments you owe and the income the property is likely to bring in so you can account for low occupancy or other unexpected costs.

7   DO YOUR DUE DILIGENCE

Investor Profile

Names: Fred and Ricardo
Property Type: Mobile Home Park/Retail Center
Famous Last Words: "If the price is right, buy right away!" and "So what if the neighborhood could change drastically? It's great right now."

*D*ue diligence is a term that comes up often in real estate, but it's surprisingly misunderstood or overlooked. Doing your due diligence means making sure all the necessary research and inspections are done before you purchase a property. You want to make sure that the property has nothing major wrong with it, or if it does, that at least you know about the issue in advance and have a plan to fix it. Due diligence also includes considering what could go wrong in the future, so you won't suddenly find yourself with a failed investment.

Fred and Ricardo were two very different investors who were both new to real estate and eager to call themselves property owners. Because they were in such a hurry and new enough not to realize all the challenges they might be up against, they skipped doing their due diligence, and this mistake was costly for both of them.

Fred and Country Hollows Mobile Home Park

Fred thought he was smart when he assembled twenty investors to buy the Country Hollows Mobile Home Park. It was a big park with over two hundred fifty units composed of all sizes of homes. The property had city water and access to city sewer lines. That was about all that it had going for it.

The property seemed like a good deal, but it was located on a slough. Water and mud kept coming up from below the streets, so it was difficult to maintain and resurface the streets of the park. The property required major construction and dewatering to make streets passable, which created significant capital expenses. In addition, Fred owned all of the electrical transformers in the park. If one failed, he had to pay to replace it rather than having the local utility companies do it for him. Over time, the transformers failed one by one, and replacing them cost over $10,000 each.

Furthermore, many of the homes were single-wide trailers versus double- or triple-wide manufactured homes. This dated the park and made it hard to attract tenants as well as buyers. Many of the tenants who were attracted to the park or who had lived there since before Fred bought it were drug dealers and other less-than-ideal tenants. One tenant was a minister who claimed he was blind and needed a seeing-eye dog. However, the on-site managers discovered him driving a van in and out of the park. Obviously, he could see, and his Great Dane was just a pet that he refused to pay pet fees for. Another tenant was a little old lady who needed to be hooked up to her oxygen tank to breathe, but she couldn't give up smoking. She lived in a very small Airstream, (aluminum) trailer, which she blew up one evening as she was smoking a cigarette. It was too close to her tank of pure, flammable oxygen. Working with the city and the DEA, it took Fred fifteen years to get rid of the bad tenants and improve the screening process. He was in a race with time because his investors were ageing and dying.

Fred, he did have a plan. He'd already addressed the slough problem, and over the next few years, he was able to replace many of the units.

Then he created a package that allowed a national mobile home park investment company to purchase the park.

Ricardo and Las Islas Verdes

Ricardo liked commercial properties. He bought a six-tenant retail strip center in Phoenix, Arizona, called Las Islas Verdes. It was located in a low-income, predominately Spanish-speaking part of town. He was able to negotiate a great deal, and he was unconcerned about the location because he spoke fluent Spanish.

Once the deal closed, Ricardo drove over to meet all the tenants. There was a *panadería* (bakery), a *supermercado* (supermarket), a café, a butcher, a flower shop, and a business where one could send money to Latin America. The building was built with Spanish-style architecture with tile roofs and stucco and brick walls.

The landscaping consisted of mostly cactus plants and green lava rock. Ricardo knew that the roof needed work and the air-conditioning systems needed to be replaced. According to the leases, the tenants were supposed to repair the rooftop-mounted air conditioning systems themselves, but they never had. Ricardo decided to replace all the air-conditioning units and have the units serviced by a landlord-administered HVAC contract. He would then bill back the tenants on a monthly basis.

All the tenants were doing pretty well, and their customers were Spanish-speaking inhabitants from the barrio, many of whom were illegal immigrants, but Ricardo was unconcerned about that. It was a neighborhood shopping center, and most people walked to the stores, just as they had in their home countries. Ricardo felt very good about investing in his community.

Then, a year later, three things happened that made Ricardo's investment go sour. First, the economy slowed down, so there were no jobs for the mostly blue-collar inhabitants of the neighborhood. Second, the state passed a law that immigrants would not be able to work without valid identification. Finally, a law was passed that immigrants would not be able to obtain a driver's license without a valid Social Security card.

The barrio emptied out. People moved to states where they could work. They had come to America to make money to send home and help support their families. With the new laws, no driver's license meant no identification, which meant no jobs, and no jobs meant no money to send home.

Because many of the teen and grown children of these illegal immigrants were legal American citizens, many of them stayed behind, but the economy was still tough, with jobs few and far between. In this barrio, these children joined gangs.

Suddenly apartment properties had 40 percent vacancy rates, and gangs were everywhere, making it unsafe to live in the neighborhood. Within a few months, the flower shop was out of business. The rest of the stores with the exception of the Super Mercado closed shortly thereafter . Ricardo had leveraged himself into the property with only 20 percent down. He never expected that the neighborhood would turn, and he felt there was not much he could do when it did. He ended up negotiating with the bank to give them the deed to the property in lieu of foreclosure. He was lucky—as an experienced businessman, he had registered his real estate investment as a limited liability company (LLC) and was able to keep from filing bankruptcy personally. He lost all of his investment in the property, though. It was a setback, but he learned from this experience and was willing to try investing in real estate again. He also kept a better lookout for factors in his investments that could fluctuate based on governmental decisions.

What Do These Two Investors Have in Common?

The moral of these two stories is that investing in real estate is not foolproof or easy. These investors made major mistakes and had to work hard to solve them. The key is not only to look at financial statements and the building during investment, but also to learn about the industry. Each real estate investment has its own set of issues. Thorough due diligence is critical. Meet with many property managers and real estate agents before you buy; they can often give you good guidance.

Lessons _____

1. A good price doesn't necessarily mean a good deal. Always do a thorough job with your due diligence so you know what kinds of issues you might face.

2. Take a good look at the tenants already on the property and the kinds of tenants who will be attracted to it. If they're not going to add value to your investment, maybe it's not the right property to invest in.

3. Even if the tenants and people in the area seem great, consider how they might change over the years.

8 OLD COMMERCIAL BUILDINGS: DUE DILIGENCE ORDEALS?

Name: Michael

Property Type: Commercial Office Building

Famous Last Words: "I have to do what, to get it up to code? No, thank you."

M ichael wanted to buy a building for his growing software development company. The Small Business Administration (SBA) financing terms at 10 percent down were incredible, and he knew that the monthly payments on a 5,000-square-foot building with the current 4 percent interest rates would be better than paying rent. He called up his broker, Clint, and said, "Let's go find a building."

They found a great building—it featured twenty parking spaces and was close to downtown as well as bus and streetcar lines. *It's perfect!* Michael thought. This edifice was built in 1924 by a well-known architect and had great character. Known as the Roman Building, it was architecturally one of a kind, with marble columns holding up the front cantilevered roof, high ceilings, large windows, and a view of the river.

Michael was enthralled. Clint told him, "Let's see how our due diligence goes."

"What's due diligence?" Michael asked.

Due Diligence

Michael and Clint walked through the building after the offer was accepted. Michael was agog with emotions, his heart beating with anticipation. Clint filled Michael in, explaining that even though Michael loved the building so far, there was still a lot to do before the sale would be final.

"In fact," Clint said, "we might even find details that make you not want to buy the building anymore." He indicated that it was time to hire the experts.

The due diligence process started. First, Clint called a structural engineer to inspect the property. He pointed out that the building was likely not up to current structural code or earthquake standards, but without a destructive test, he could not confirm the construction methodology. He would need to rip out some sheetrock to view the structural components, he said. Michael shook his head, horrified at the destruction the test would cause.

Next, the HVAC technician came out. He reported that the HVAC system was almost sixty years old, was wrapped in asbestos, and would be impossible to find replacement parts for. He also indicated that the heating in the building had originally been sawdust and wood, was later converted to coal, and was now an oil-burning furnace, with the oil tank buried in the basement floor. The technician questioned if the tank had leaked, given its age, and suggested that Michael get a pressure test performed on it. Air- conditioning was nonexistent—well, unless you included the fifty-year- old abandoned swamp cooler located in the attic crawl space.

When the surveyor came to the site, she discovered that part of the building was located on city property, not just on the property Michael would own. Clint explained that this meant Michael would have to negotiate with the city to restructure the property lines, which could be costly.

Despite the expensive news regarding the structural integrity, HVAC system, and property lines, Michael was still hopeful, so he and Clint continued with the due diligence. They brought in a building inspector to determine if the building was at risk for dry rot, pests, or problems with basic building operation. The inspector found extensive dry rot as well as carpenter ants, and he reported that the water lines were galvanized iron instead of copper or Pex pipe and were leaking. He also took color photos that showed mildew and mold, not to mention nuts left by the squirrels in the attic. The chimney needed to be tuck-pointed, and the siding needed to be sealed to keep the rain and wind out. The window frames were rotten to the core.

The window sashes were worn out, and the windows had to be held open with wooden broom handles cut to size. He also noted that the lighting system in the building was very old and might not comply with current codes. On the way out, he suggested that Michael get the sewer line inspected.

When Michael did that, he discovered that the sewer lines were the originals from 1924—and they had been destroyed by roots of the nearby ninety-year-old trees. It was a miracle that the sewage still drained.

The inspector also pointed out that the building bathrooms were not compliant with the Americans with Disabilities Act (ADA). The restrooms were very small, clearly added as an afterthought. The entryway to the building wasn't ADA compliant either, as there was no wheelchair ramp for handicap access.

The building inspector mentioned the parking lot in his report too. There were no handicapped parking spaces, which were required by law. Not only that, but the entire parking lot was in major need of an asphalt overlay, seal coating, and striping. He also mentioned that the drain in the parking lot was attached to a dry well, which was illegal in that part of town. All parking lot drains needed to be connected to storm sewer lines and retrofitted with special filtering systems.

The building inspector suggested that Michael have the roof inspected. The roofing inspector looked at the Franvisa Spanish black slate roof and gave it a twenty-year certification. The roof was as solid as a rock. Clint nodded happily at this news, and Michael would have felt relieved if it weren't for all the bad news they were getting.

Because the building was a two story, it also had a fire escape. Due to the age of the building, though, there was no sprinkler system. And unfortunately, the fire escape had been red-tagged by the fire marshal because the landing was rusted out.

Finally, Michael and Clint called an inspector for the elevator and found out that it, too, was not up to code and most likely needed replacement. Unfortunately, it sounded like Michael's dream building had not been occupied for fifty of the ninety or so years since the building had been built and it had not been taken care of.

Faced with the long and expensive laundry list of needed repairs, Michael was no longer in love with the Roman Building. He turned to Clint after the last inspector left and said, "Okay, I give up. Can we find a more modern building that doesn't have so many warts?"

Black Cloud with a Silver Lining

Due diligence does not end with inspections, though, and Clint told Michael not to give up. It sounded like the perfect building for him, having location, easy access, parking, and a classic design.

Clint reminded him, "In real estate, location is everything, and for the right location, many investors have renovated in the face of countless old- building issues to produce a gem with value that far exceeded their initial investment and improvement expenses."

Now he had Michael's attention. Clint advised that whenever an old building is acquired, there are always several issues that arise with that building's condition. But first, a prospective purchaser has to ask, what will the building be used for? And another equally important question is, what can be done to mitigate upgrade costs? If the building, because of its condition, is being acquired at a low cost per square foot, and the cost per square foot to upgrade can be estimated, then it is easy to decide if the property is worth the investment.

Each professional doing due diligence inspections has a responsibility to report issues to the prospective client. Some are better than others at doing so but drawing a clear picture of the condition of the building is important.

Clint explained to Michael, "The consultant is always going to say that the building isn't up to current code. Codes change all the time, so the truth is, hardly any buildings are up to code." Michael learned that the question is not if a building is up to current code, but rather if it is required to be up to code. Just because codes have changed doesn't mean that everything in current code must be implemented into existing buildings.

Then Clint walked Michael through the list of specific items reported on the Roman Building inspections.

Structure: Clint told Michael he didn't need to be scared of the destructive investigation the engineer needed to do—the damage could be repaired. They needed to ask the engineer to make a worst-case estimate of costs to mitigate structural issues based on what he knew about the building. HVAC: Clint drew on his real estate experience to point out that the HVAC issues sounded far worse than they likely were, especially since Michael wanted to air-condition the building. A new heat pump system would provide everything he needed and reduce his operating expenses at the same time. The asbestos could be managed in place, so immediate mitigation would not be required. Clint said the oil tank situation needed to be examined further. It might not be leaking, and if it was, it could be decommissioned in place. Proper testing would involve drilling for soil samples near the tank, but again, this destruction could be repaired.

Handicap accessibility: ADA is a big issue, but not all buildings are necessarily required to meet it, and folks have come to expect that some buildings will not be accessible. Clint filled Michael in that when he applied for a construction permit to remodel, he would be required to spend a percentage of his renovation budget on ADA improvements, but he didn't necessarily have to address all the issues the inspector brought up when it came to ADA.

Parking lot: The parking lot may have needed to be resurfaced, but there are ways to mitigate the cost of resurfacing a parking lot. For instance, cutting out bad spots, patching them, and then slurry coating the entire lot might be a really good solution for a third of the cost of a new lot. The drain could be dealt with by installing approved filter units directly into the catch basins and servicing them according to a regular schedule. Once the lot was redone, it would be easy to install the minimum required ADA parking space.

Fire escape: To solve the fire escape problem, Michael could consider adding an interior stairway for exiting, thereby eliminating the need for an exterior escape, especially if he was going to remodel the building anyway. Elevator: Clint let Michael in on a secret that most first-time investors don't know: "Elevator code is so strict; most elevators don't meet it." The important thing for Michael was that his be repaired, licensed, and on a regular service contract. Even when an elevator has outlived its useful life, there is a lot that can be done to improve it and make it fully serviceable again without installing a new one.

Hearing all this, Michael was relieved. Clint had taken what felt like an impossible situation and given Michael hope that he really could have the beautiful historic building he envisioned for his business. Together, Clint and Michael went about obtaining bids for each of the repairs and upgrades, and they ultimately discovered that upgrading the Roman Building would cost substantially less than buying a modern building that met all the codes and was in a great central city location. Michael decided to buy and remodel the Roman Building.

Lessons _____

1. First, hire a knowledgeable real estate professional.

2. Get licensed professionals to complete all the inspections so you know who you're dealing with, but don't be scared off by the results.

3. Before you decide not to buy an old building, understand how much you really need to upgrade and then compare the costs of upgrading versus buying a new building.

9 LOCATION, LOCATION, LOCATION

Investor Profile

Names: James and Marshall
Property Type: Apartments
Famous Last Words: "A little friendly competition will be fun. Let's see who can buy and renovate the most successful apartments."

J ames and Marshall were good friends but the sort who liked to compete. They were old college roommates, and they'd always had an unspoken competition on who could take the most rigorous classes, who could win more sports honors, who could drive the nicer car, and who could buy the bigger TV. Now, though, the stakes had gotten higher. They were competing with real estate and would see who could develop the more successful apartment building.

James and the South Waterton Apartments

James purchased a forty-five-unit apartment building in the South Waterton district. It was a great deal at only $20,000 a unit. There were 20 one-bedroom units and 25 two-bedroom units, all very spacious but also very old.

This 1920s property was a great deal indeed—a great deal of work.

None of the bedrooms or bathrooms had more than one electrical outlet. The building still used fuses, which blew constantly. Anyone experienced in real estate could see that the seller was getting out of this deal because it was a maintenance money pit.

James, on the other hand, thought he was getting a deal. He had run the numbers. Even if the building burned down, he was happy with the deal. South Waterton was in the path of growth, and it was still an affordable part of town. James was thinking of a total renovation of the building using either a HUD (FHA) Section 221(d) rehabilitation loan or a HUD (FHA) 223(f) acquisition loan. These loans, commonly available through Housing and Urban Development (HUD), were focused on keeping housing affordable, and had thirty-five- to forty-year terms, plenty of time for James to pay off the debt.

Marshall and the North Waterton Manor

Marshall found a property in North Waterton, on Monty Street. This fifty-six-unit property was all brick, built in 1957. All the units were two bedrooms and heated with a central heat boiler. The electrical was based on breaker boxes. The building was empty and boarded up and had not been inhabited for five years.

Marshall bought the property for $10,000 per unit, half of what James paid per unit on his building. The bank that owned the property carried the financing and needed to get the property off its books. Marshall was excited, so he started renovations immediately. He wanted his building to be ready before James's South Waterton Apartments were.

But Marshall ran into problems. He thought the building was empty, but a drug kingpin had set up operations at the property and was not happy about being evicted. The police told Marshall that the crime in that part of town was 50 percent higher than anywhere else, so he had to hire a private police force to make sure the remodeling contractors were safe, and the renovation supplies would not be stolen from the worksite. Of course, he had not included security expenses in his reconstruction budget.

Finally, the day came for Marshall to start renting units. But every potential tenant had a criminal record or did not qualify to rent the property. Marshall had not expected that the potential tenants would not be able to qualify to rent his apartment units. He probably should have, though, since the rest of Monty Street was also boarded up. Marshall recognized that he needed help.

James's Renovation Woes

When James went to pull a permit, he was told the building was listed on the National Register of Historic Places. Therefore, he could only make renovations that were in line with historical standards if he wanted to keep the tax abatements that he'd been expecting.

These restrictions were a major snag, so James hired a consultant with experience in historical building construction and tax abatements. The consultant told him, "To be eligible for the property tax abatement on the cost of rehabilitating an income-producing building, several things have to happen." He then gave James a five-part list:

1. The building must be in a historic district listed in the national register, or it must be individually listed on the register.
2. The building must be historic, meaning it was built before the end of the period of significance for the district.
3. It must still be recognizable as historic, not remodeled into something else.
4. Historic rehabilitation guidelines must be followed on both the interior and exterior renovations.
5. Twenty-four to thirty-six photos of the existing building must be submitted with the application.

These additional parameters were unexpected, but James stuck with it. All his units had a view of the local lake, and he knew he would come out okay if he could create a modern yet traditional feel.

The building was five stories high and had an old elevator. He installed a new elevator and made sure all the units had up-to-date heating and air-conditioning. In addition, he completely replumbed and rewired the building and added security features. He also bought two small retail buildings nearby and renovated them and leased them out to create a buzz in the neighborhood.

Marshall Gives Up

Marshall saw that James was running into roadblocks with his project, but at least there was a future in South Waterton. As he looked at North Waterton, he decided there was no future and he needed to cut his losses.

First, he approached a community development corporation to see if it would help him by developing surrounding properties. They indicated interest, but their lead times were two years out. Then he approached a nonprofit group composed of successful developers who pooled resources to redevelop dilapidated homes on one street at a time, but they did not have money to help.

Marshall decided his best option was to sell the building. He approached low-income housing providers, such as Volunteers of America and the local Housing Authority. Volunteers of America loved the renovations to the building, and it had tenants who could move in. The organization planned to form a separate nonprofit that would run the building. Marshall was happy he could sell the building without going bankrupt.

James Succeeds Due to His Superior Location

James's project was finally finished. He rented all the units in four months and made a positive impact on the neighborhood. It cost him more than he'd expected, but he had a gorgeous building to show for it, in a neighborhood that was turning in his favor. His location was superior to Marshall's location and created significant tangible and intangible benefits, something to consider with real estate investment.

Lessons _____

1. Make sure your real estate investment fits the character of the neighborhood you are investing in.

2. When you run into a snag—and you probably will—seek professional help to see if there are resources you do not know about yet.

3. Remember, it's about location, location, location first—but also term, timing, and government regulations.

10 MAKING SURE YOUR FINANCIALS ARE EASY TO FOLLOW

Investor Profile

Names: Suzie and Charles
Property Type: Houses
Famous Last Words: "Bookkeeping isn't really necessary. Everything balances itself out in the end."

Suzie and Charles, a wife-and-husband team, had been investing in houses for years. Usually they bought an investment, renovated it, and sold it to another buyer within 120 days. One day, their financial planner suggested they keep a few of their investment properties. He pointed out that a recent trend for builders was to construct a few buildings for clients and then build one to keep in their personal portfolio and rent it out. That way, they built a retirement fund and increased their net worth. The same concept could apply to Suzie and Charles too.

Charles and Suzie liked the idea and decided their goal would be to keep every fifth property they purchased. An interesting side effect of their plan was that their net worth started climbing faster, and banks were more interested in doing business with them.

Although the couple had friends who raved about how much easier renting was when they hired a property management company, Charles and Suzie decided that they wanted to manage the properties themselves.

Challenges of Bookkeeping

On their first project, a three-bedroom house, things were pretty easy for Suzie and Charles: one tenant, one deposit, one rent. But as they started adding properties, it became confusing.

They had not set up separate accounts for the rental properties and had mixed up the rental funds with income from their company. When their CPA objected and suggested separate accounts, they instead shifted their rental funds over to their personal account, thinking it would be easier to monitor. Of course, they used credit cards, debit cards, and checks to pay their bills. Since the account always had a positive balance when they looked online, they thought they were on top of it all. Then they purchased another house and also ran it through the family checkbook.

At the end of the first year, the first tenant needed to move and wanted her security deposit back. Suzie, who'd been doing the bookkeeping, wrote a check to the tenant and promptly received an overdraft notice. She scurried to the bank to find out what the problem was and discovered that yes, indeed, she had overdrawn the account. She assumed Charles must have written a large check or paid a bill with the debit card and she just didn't know about it. She didn't worry and simply transferred money from reserve funds to cover the tenant's deposit check.

Suzie hurried home and thought about reconciling the account. But that was a job she hated, so she didn't do it. She also forgot to mention to Charles that the account was overdrawn.

A month later the tenant in the second rental moved out. Once again, Suzie wrote the security deposit refund check; she was faced with another overdraft. This time she did discuss it with Charles.

"I don't know, sweetie," he said. "I didn't write any big checks. I'm sure it's just a little mishap and it won't happen again."

Suzie nodded. To admit it might be more than a little mishap would be to acknowledge that she wasn't recording the finances very well. Besides, she much preferred the excitement of buying and renovating the next property over crunching the numbers. She transferred the money from reserve funds again and didn't think about it anymore.

A CPA's Nightmare

At the end of the year, Charles and Suzie's CPA asked for all the income and expense records for the house renovation and flipping business, personal bills, and rental investments so he could prepare their taxes.

They brought him the proverbial shoebox of bills and receipts. He was not happy. He told them they needed to separate all the income and invoices before he would touch their tax return. So, Suzie and Charles planned to spend one weekend sorting out their accounts. They worked on defining what was a deposit and what was a rent check, what was a deposit refund and what was a check for rental bills as well as checks for personal bills.

But the weekend wasn't enough time. After five days, Charles said, "I've had enough! There has to be a better way." He and Suzie went back to their CPA and asked for help.

Their CPA told them that they needed a separate account for their personal expenses, one for each property they managed, and one for their flipping business. He also told them they had to reconcile all of these accounts every month to make sure everything balanced.

They groaned.

"That would be five different accounts," Suzie whined. "And that's just for right now—imagine after we keep investing!" She already had trouble just keeping up with depositing and writing checks, and reconciling the accounts felt tantamount to sitting in a prison cell.

"Relax," the CPA said. "I'll set up the accounting software for you and show you how to keep it up so it's easy."

Separate Books

Suzie and Charles hired their CPA to set up their accounting system. Then they realized how much easier it was to keep separate books. They actually made a consistent profit because they could easily track rental bills now instead of losing them in the morass of personal and company bills. They knew exactly how much profit they were making each month and could make calculated decisions about what money to spend on personal expenses and new investments. For the first time, the couple could run the rental side of their business without stress. It helped that they hired a local bookkeeper to post the bills, write the checks, and reconcile their accounts. All they had to do to stay on top of the books was sign the checks and review the work completed by the bookkeeper.

In addition, their CPA was finally able to prepare their taxes correctly, and they were able to qualify for tax deductions that they didn't even know existed from their rental investments. As side effects of this process, they could better plan their investments, build a solid net worth, and accumulate a stable retirement fund. As a result, Suzie and Charles were able to plan a trip to Mexico to celebrate the solution to their financial problems.

Lessons _____

1. Never mix up your business and personal bank accounts.

2. Have a good accounting system in place. It seems like a lot of work at first, but it's much easier in the long run.

3. If a task like bookkeeping feels too hard for you to figure out, ask an expert to explain it to you. It will save you a lot of stress!

11 EXIT STRATEGY: AN OFTEN-FORGOTTEN RULE

Investor Profile

Names: Toni and Jason

Property Type: First Investment

Famous Last Words: "All that matters is to start, right? Exit strategies are just extra work."

Toni and her husband, Jason, were at a lavish cocktail party to celebrate the seventy-fifth anniversary for the local art museum. All the big players in the art world were at this event, as were the big donors. Toni and Jason had already viewed the new contemporary art exhibit and were now in the museum's ballroom for the cocktail party. They saw several movie stars among the crowd, and they were sure many of the other attendees were either artists featured at the museum or big donors.

"Look, there's Leonardo DiCaprio." Toni pointed discreetly. "I heard he has a whole new house he's been filling with contemporary art."

Jason nodded and pointed out some of the big donors for the museum too. Toni and Jason were considered bronze-level donors—they supported the museum with an annual financial contribution, but they were nowhere near the level of movie stars. They were excited and inspired to be in such illustrious company.

When Jason saw an old friend and went over to catch up, Toni decided she would introduce herself to some of the other people in the room.

As she made her way around the ballroom looking for a good conversation to join, she quickly discovered that nearly everyone was discussing where to invest—commodities, real estate, diamonds, and so on—because the stock market was slow. Toni was visiting with her acquaintances and friends when she overheard a conversation between two real estate investors and perked up. She and Jason had been wanting to invest in real estate, but they weren't sure if the market was quite right. She overheard that the older one, Reinhardt, was assembling a real estate fund and was using this event to find investors for his next venture.

The younger one, Jonah, was president of a successful manufacturer of heart stents and valves, and he was looking for a place to invest.

Toni positioned herself close to them. Reinhardt was discussing his philosophy regarding real estate investments and was illustrating it with a short story, so Toni listened closely.

Reinhardt's Philosophy

Reinhardt began his story: "Early in my career, I partnered up with a few other investors and bought a fifty-unit apartment property on the coast in San Diego. It really didn't have much cash flow, but you know the strength of the San Diego economy: the military, the military contractors, and people emigrating from Latin America. We felt it was a straightforward play." Reinhardt took a sip from his martini and then went on.

"The plan was to get in and get out five years later. Unfortunately, five years later the economy was miserable, and we couldn't find a buyer no matter what we tried. It was a hard lesson for me. My partners were furious, and some were desperate for cash, but I was able to convince them to hang in there for about three more years when we sold at a breakeven point. We invest very differently now."

Toni was nearly distracted by more movie stars moving through the crowd, but she was extremely curious about Reinhardt's new approach to investing. She thought maybe she could learn from his mistake and be more likely to succeed than most new investors.

"Now my partners and I set the goal to have more than one exit strategy if we can. Sometimes we get locked in by financing and end up with an interest-only conduit loan that is hard to assume. We try to set up deals with the maximum amount of flexibility. The market is just that—a marketplace that continually changes due to outside and often unfathomable influences." That made sense to Toni, but she was not sure what exactly to do with that little tidbit.

Jonah apparently felt the same way. "That's an interesting perspective, but what can you really do to control your circumstances in an uncontrollable market?"

"It's all about having more than one exit strategy." Reinhardt made it sound so simple. "For example, six years ago we purchased an industrial park that looked like a great investment at face value. All the buildings were rented. We had hoped to paint, redecorate, and turn the property. Then one of the tenants with stellar credit closed their business. They were in two of the six buildings. That put us into a negative cash flow position. Our first exit strategy to just focus on redecorating and selling wouldn't work because buyers don't want to invest in property that's only two- thirds rented and has a negative cash flow. We needed a new exit strategy to make the property appeal to buyers."

That sounded complicated. Toni sipped her cocktail and noticed that other people were starting to listen in on Reinhardt's story too.

"So, what we did, was replat the business park and sell off the buildings individually," Reinhardt explained. "In order to do this, we had to form a condominium association because utilities, driveways, and other common areas were shared. We were lucky that this was a light industrial park because otherwise there might have been some thorny hazardous waste that we would've had to clean up. We actually made more money than we had planned because the empty buildings were bought by two owner- users, and we didn't have to prelease to sell the buildings."

Reinhardt finally noticed the crowd that was building up and smiled at Toni and the others.

Jonah asked, "Isn't it pretty rare for an exit strategy like that to work out, though?"

"Actually, no," Reinhardt answered. "We did the same thing with a 126-unit apartment complex. That property was made up of four-, six-, and eight-plex properties, so we managed it as apartments for a while. Then we slowly phased out of the property, one building at a time, and did very well. The challenge here and in the commercial industrial park was financing and negotiating with the banks to allow us to sell the buildings one at a time. In the second case, we obtained a lot-release loan that let us sell one property at a time. In the first case, we had to do a lot of begging, and in the end we had to pay down the loan first before we could distribute money to any of the partners."

Toni's Takeaway

Jason joined Toni with two fresh glasses of champagne and caviar canapés. "This guy's looking for investors and sounds like he's got a lot of experience," Toni filled him in. "The other guy is thinking about doing it." Meanwhile, Jonah responded, "Each of those situations requires repositioning assets and waiting years, though." He sipped, letting that observation sink in. Toni noticed a few people in the crowd nodding. "That just sounds risky to me. Can't I put my money into a short-term real estate investment, much like a stock or bond, and be out in less than a year?"

Reinhardt shook his head. "We've never really had much luck with investments held for less than five years. The costs of purchasing, repositioning, and selling consume a lot of the increase in cash flow, which would not be available to pay to our partners. We need a longer term to make real estate pay off for our investors, and most of our clients like the fact that real estate is in fact tangible. They can drive by and see it if they want to. Plus, it's favorable on your taxes because you can also receive depreciation shelter as part of your return."

"That's a lot to think about." Jonah looked crestfallen. "I need to rejoin my wife, but please give me your business card, and I will follow up during the week." He drifted back to the party.

Reinhardt turned to Toni and Jason. "I see you've been watching and listening. Are you potential investors?"

Toni explained that she and Jason had been on the lookout for the right circumstances to make their first real estate investment.

Reinhardt smiled encouragingly. "As you heard, real estate investment is tricky and needs to be thought about on many levels. Many people say that you make money buying the investment, not selling it. I always say it's best to strategize your purchase so that you're protected. You should plan to make money on both the buying and the selling end of a real estate transaction, so if something goes wrong, you have multiple exit strategies to consider."

Toni and Jason were impressed. "We'll take one of your business cards too." As they left the art museum, Toni and Jason excitedly chatted about the possibilities. They'd had their eye on a retail center but were wary of investing all on their own. Reinhardt's new project seemed like a good option to consider—plus, they'd have an expert calling the shots, so they'd feel secure but could also continue to learn from him.

Lessons _____

1. Have an exit strategy before you purchase.

2. Your exit strategies are just as important as what you choose to invest in.

3. Always have at least two exit strategies in mind when it comes to real estate and be prepared to come up with a different one if your circumstances change.

12 THE WRONG ATTORNEY

Name: Gus
Property Type: Ranch
Famous Last Words: "I know a good attorney when I see one. No interview necessary."

G us was a farmer who owned six thousand acres divided among four farms near Anaconda in western Montana. Morris, his attorney for the previous twenty years, notified him, "You know I'm seventy-five and need to retire. It's time for you to find another attorney."

Gus wasn't surprised. Morris had advised him well over the years, and he was glad to see him settling into retirement. Gus's problem was that there were only two attorneys in town, and he didn't get along with the other one. So, he drove to Butte to find another.

He checked into Eddy's Motel, and the next morning he visited four attorneys. He liked one named Robert Whitehat very much, especially because Gus had met Robert's uncle at a rodeo years ago. "How's he doing now?" Gus asked.

"Well, he's pretty stove up from all the bones he broke over the years," Robert said. "But he still manages to hunt every fall."

Gus smiled. "Well, tell me, what kind of experience do you have as an attorney?" He wasn't sure what answer he was looking for since his father had simply told him to work with Morris all those years ago, but he figured it was something he should ask.

Robert explained that most of his experience was with wills and estates. This sounded good enough to Gus. Robert Whitehat took over as Gus's attorney.

The Ranch Keeps Growing

Gus kept buying real estate, and the size of his ranch grew to ten thousand acres. He had become a big rancher. Robert encouraged him with every purchase, and he sent him an article from a local newspaper that covered interesting Montana facts:

- Montana has 60 million acres of farm and ranch land, ranking it number two in the nation for acreage farmed.
- Montana ranches average 2,210 acres, making it number four in the country for size of farms.
- There are 28,300 farms and ranches in Montana.
- Individuals, family partnerships, or family corporations own 98 percent of ranches and farms in the country.
- Each farmer in Montana produces enough food to feed about 144 people per year.

Gus felt like a big shot. Statistically he was a leading rancher in the country, and he was sure his assets would grow as time went on.

As Gus neared sixty, Robert had been his attorney for nearly fifteen years and had helped him get through a divorce, set up a will, and manage other life changes. Now Gus decided he would consolidate some of his assets closer to home and sell a four-hundred-acre parcel. When he received an offer from an adjoining rancher, it was a fair price, so Gus agreed to sell. He informed Robert of the situation, and everything seemed to be moving along smoothly. However, when the legal documents arrived, Gus noticed that something did not look right. Robert didn't seem to be asking the right questions.

The Attorney Did Not Protect His Client

Gus had noticed that Morris, his old attorney, had always asked about water rights, easements, leases with the Bureau of Land Management and the Forest Service, and American Land Title Association (ALTA) surveys.

Robert, however, just put the deal in the hands of the escrow company, and the Realtor didn't ask any of these questions either. What made Gus even more nervous was a question regarding the way Gus had bought the property originally. At the time, Gus had been married, and his wife was a partner in the property, but that had been ten years ago. Her name should not have been showing up on documents anymore; the divorce should have taken care of that. Unfortunately, Robert had not made the changes to the appropriate documents when Gus got his divorce.

Now Gus had to go to his ex-wife to get her permission to sell the property and her agreement to the sale price. She smiled. "All right, I'll sign the paperwork, but only in exchange for a portion of the sale proceeds."

Gus finally realized he had hired an attorney with no real estate or divorce experience. He was furious with himself.

Gus Finds the Right Attorney

Gus needed an attorney with real estate experience. He asked all his friends and ranching buddies, and they recommended two firms, one of which he chose. He decided not to sell the four-hundred-acre parcel and instead worked with the new attorney, Sam, to backtrack through all his properties and holding companies to fix all the details that Robert had overlooked over the years. This cost Gus thousands of dollars, but it was better than waiting and wondering what other major problems he might face in the future.

Gus realized that as a large rancher, he needed to spend more time with his attorney, so he planned a quarterly lunch with Sam. In addition, they agreed that there would be a backup attorney from the firm who would go to lunch with them and keep up on Gus's dealings. Gus felt that way he could better protect himself in case Sam retired too.

Beyond that, Gus decided that once a year, he would consult a tax attorney with Sam just to test his ideas, get second opinions, and plan his purchase and sale decisions. By now, Gus's older son had become the ranch manager and was also involved in the meetings. The ranch was getting bigger and bigger, and it was easy to make a mistake—a costly mistake. Gus did not want to do that again.

Gus ended up paying his ex-wife payments to ensure her cooperation in future land deals. He still loved ranching and the art of the real estate deal, and in his older age, he was learning how to manage better, especially how to choose and manage his attorney.

Lessons _____

1. Do not just hire the first attorney who comes along. Choose an attorney with good references and real estate experience, especially the kind of real estate you are working in.

2. Double-check all legal documents to make sure your attorney is asking the right questions and that there aren't mistakes.

13 SEALED WITH A HANDSHAKE

Investor Profile

Name: Chris
Property Type: Commercial Office Building
Famous Last Words: "Dad was a good investor. If a handshake was good enough for him, should it be for me too?"

The door on the downtown Chicago office read "Church and Lefkowitz Real Estate Investments." Chris was there to see Jacob Lefkowitz, the managing partner of the real estate partnership in which his father had invested $200,000. As Chris entered the office, he was impressed by the view of Lake Michigan. The office had been in the Board of Trade Building for thirty years, always on the top floor, always with the beautiful view. Jacob was seventy years old and had been investing in real estate for fifty years.

Chris's father had been a partner with him for forty of those years, and they had invested in many properties together. Over the last few years of his life, Chris's father had sold off his interests apart from this last one, a stake in the American Surprise Building. Chris's father had deeded his investments to him, and he was there that morning because there was a problem.

The Problem

The problem was that Chris's father and Jacob had made the deal on a handshake over thirty years ago, and there were no records stating that they had been co-investors in the American Surprise Building. What was clear was the investment amount; what was not clear was how much the children, like Chris, would receive if they wanted to get out of the partnership, because there was no written agreement.

Chris liked Jacob and his daughter, Abigail, but preferred the stock market to real estate and wanted to redeploy the money. Jacob welcomed Chris into his office—he knew why he was visiting. His daughter, Abigail, joined them as well.

"I miss your father," Jacob said. "We were the best of friends, and we made a lot of money together, always on a handshake."

Chris grunted an acknowledgment.

Jacob then handed the floor over to Abigail, who started with a rundown of the building's current income and expenses, a review of the past twelve months, and a preview of the future.

Jacob cleared his throat. "I know you want to sell your interest and get out of this investment. I'd like to make two comments in that regard. First, we have just filled the building, and with a series of rent increases, the value of the property is going to increase by 15 percent in the next twelve months. The existing partners do not have the cash to buy your interest. If you want your 40 percent interest now, we'd have to liquidate the property."

Chris was floored; he had no idea that his father held a 40 percent interest in the American Surprise Building.

Jacob continued that the current value of the building was $39 million, but if they waited twelve months, it would be worth close to $45 million. That got Chris's attention.

But Chris was suspicious, especially with that much money at stake. He asked Jacob and Abigail, "How do you know we own 40 percent of the building?"

Abigail answered, "We have records of the withdrawals and bank loans that have notations to that effect. In addition, your father bought out three of the original partners with cash he had from liquidating other real estate investments he and my father had partnered up on. We have records of those transactions."

Being the cautious fellow that Chris was, he asked to see those documents. Abigail hemmed and hawed and sputtered, "They're in a storage locker and will take a while to produce." She asked for ten days, and Chris agreed.

Ten Days Later

Chris returned to Church and Lefkowitz with his CPA, Maxwell. Abigail greeted him at the door and took him into the main conference room where stacks of papers were laid out on the table. Abigail handed him a small booklet. "This is the map of the trail of the transactions that led to your father's share of the partnership. It's convoluted. I would ask you to be patient with the materials. Many of them are over twenty-five years old and are hard to read."

So, Maxwell and Chris went to work. They studied all day and the next day too. Finally, Maxwell pronounced, "It looks like Church and Lefkowitz treated your father fairly. That's quite an accomplishment, especially without a written agreement. You really do own 40 percent of the American Surprise Building."

Chris went to Abigail's office. "Okay, I'm convinced, and I want to share in the upside, but I don't want to continue further on just a handshake." Abigail agreed. "Let's move into the twenty-first century and formalize our handshake agreement with a written partnership agreement."

The Agreement

They drafted an agreement that defined these key issues:

1. The members of the partnership
2. How and when to sell and who needed to agree to the sale of the property
3. What would happen if a partner filed for bankruptcy
4. What would happen if a partner faced divorce or passed away

5. How shares would be valued if a partner wanted to sell

6. Priority to sell to the other partners first

7. Permission to allow Church and Lefkowitz to choose the management agent

8. A stipulation of monthly financial reports

9. A set date for an annual meeting and review of progress

10. An agreement for an annual audit of operations and financial statements

11. An agreement to share the depreciation with Chris, particularly depreciation created by tenant improvements

Abigail and Jacob had convinced Chris that he would make more money in this real estate investment. He went along for the time being, feeling more comfortable now because they had a written agreement.

He knew this agreement was a critical piece of their partnership. Just the week before, he had heard a story from a friend about two developers who owned an apartment property together. One was in serious financial trouble and wanted to sell the asset to generate cash. The other partner was not ready to sell and was stalling. He did not have the money to buy out the troubled partner, but it was a great property and he needed time to sort out his options. Meanwhile, the troubled partner was marketing the property. They ended up suing each other. It was not a good situation. Chris was lucky to have good partners whom he could trust.

Lessons _____

1. Our parents and grandparents did business differently, but that doesn't protect you in today's world. When you inherit property, update agreements to modern standard practices.

2. A partnership agreement should be in writing and should detail not just expectations of each partner but also under what circumstances the ownership can change.

14 OUT OF CASH

Investor Profile

Name: Marta
Property Type: Small Real Estate Investments
Famous Last Words: "When you run out of money, consider a hard money lender to solve a short-term problem."

Marta was an aggressive real estate investor. She invested every last dime in her properties. As her properties grew, she regularly harvested their equity through refinancing and reinvesting into other properties.

This strategy worked fine until Marta fell in love with a cute, Spanish-style fourplex in her favorite part of town. The architecture was exquisite and unique in the marketplace. Properties like this didn't come on the market very often. These attributes prompted Marta to overpay for the new property even though she was in the middle of a major renovation on an apartment building she recently purchased only months before, but she had no reservations about this decision. The fourplex was a class A property with several recent upgrades, so Marta figured the purchase wouldn't stress the budget she had set aside to renovate her fixer property.

Boiling Over

Among the recent upgrades, the original boiler had been retrofitted, at great expense, to use natural gas instead of coal, or heating oil, as it had been originally designed. Barely two months after her purchase, the boiler failed despite the updates the previous owner had made. Marta's phone was ringing off the hook as all her tenants were calling to complain. She became even more distraught when she called the furnace repair company—they wanted to be paid cash, but Marta didn't have reserves and her credit card was maxed out, as she had used her credit line to help pay the down payment to purchase this property.

Stuck

Marta was in love with the property, but the stress due to the boiler was making her sick. She called her CPA, her bank, and her attorney to see if they had any ideas. The bank told her they could put a second mortgage on her house and lend her the $20,000 she needed with 10 annual percent interest amortized over ten years but payable in five years. The CPA suggested hard money lenders. These lenders would take more risk but wanted 6 percent loan fee up front and 15 percent annual interest.

Marta knew she was running out of time to make a decision. Her attorney told her he would lend her the money for 10 percent interest and 2 percent loan fee but in exchange, he wanted a 10 percent interest in the property. Marta liked her attorney, but she did not want a partner. So, she opted for the bank's proposal.

It took twenty-four hours for the bank to originate the loan. In the meantime, Marta put her tenants up in a nearby hotel. Finally, she had the money and the appointment with the furnace repair company.

The Continuing Search for Money

Her relief was short lived. The contractor renovating her fixer apartment building had been trying to talk her into replacing the roof in addition to the cosmetic updates already underway. She penciled his quote into her long-term plan but decided to put if off for the time being.

Then one day he called to report leaks that she couldn't ignore. If she didn't repair the roof now, she could potentially ruin all the updates she was already paying for. She was already overextended from her new property, and she could not get long-term, low-interest financing without the new roof.

Marta called her bank for a short-term credit line, but this time the bank said no—not without a functioning roof.

What to do? Marta was desperate for cash. She called, emailed, and texted her friends, her real estate agent, and her CPA for suggestions to help her find money. They suggested she find a hard money lender.

Marta wanted to learn more about this option before, so she scheduled a lunch meeting with her real estate agent, Sheryl.

She pulled into the Applebee's parking lot with a lot on her mind. She really needed to find a solution to her roofing problem, which, of course was linked to a lack-of-money problem. If she could just get enough cash to fix that roof, she could refinance that house and then start to build up her cash reserves from all her properties. Maybe working with a hard money lender as everyone suggested would help her with this, but she wasn't sure. *What if they take advantage of me and I end up losing money?* She decided it was time to find out. She pulled her purse over her shoulder and headed into the restaurant.

Sheryl had been advising Marta for about five years, and Marta knew she could trust her. She was just concerned that she'd gotten herself into an unresolvable situation. Sheryl quickly calmed Marta's concerns, though. After they'd ordered their food, Sheryl explained that hard money lenders fill a very specific need for short-term money: they lend for up to two years. They expect their borrowers to pay back the money in that time, either by refinancing through conventional sources or selling the real estate they've been renovating, remodeling, or constructing.

"That seems like it would work perfectly for my situation," Marta said.

Sheryl nodded. "It could." She went on to explain, hard money lenders come in many forms. Often, they are private investors who have cash they want to put to work in short-term investments at higher-than-market return rates. Hard money can also be borrowed from hard money brokers. They tend to act as conduits to private investors who have the money. These brokers do the loan sourcing, screening, and documentation for the investors.

After they paid for their food, Sheryl wrapped up her explanation. "A few of my other clients have worked with Pat from Premier Lending," she said. "From what I hear, he works with private investors and uses a bank credit line to get cash for his investor clients. Typically, he turns around a short-term loan in two weeks or less." Marta gladly accepted Pat's contact information. "Of course, do your research and talk to other hard money lenders too before making a decision," Sheryl warned.

When Marta called Pat, he quoted a 5 percent loan origination fee and a significantly high interest rate. He also wanted to secure his loan position with a first trust deed so that if Marta didn't pay him back promptly, he could take the property, complete the renovation project if necessary, and then sell it to recover his position. Marta followed Sheryl's advice and contacted some other hard money lenders too.

One offered her detailed terms in an email, which Marta liked because it was in writing and she could refer back to it. The terms included:

- Loans are short-term with a two-year maximum
- Interest rates and points vary by region, loan conditions, and transaction type
- Rate: 10%–16%
- Prepaid Interest: 90–180 days
- Minimum Loan Amount: $50,000
- Maximum Loan Amount: $1 million
- Exit Strategy: Must have a well-researched plan for resale or refinance
- Additional fees include document preparation and appraisal fee paid by borrower

While there were some details about this that Marta liked, she also felt like it was not quite the right fit, mainly because she didn't quite need $50,000 for a roof and because she didn't want to pay the up-front appraisal and document preparation fees. Marta decided to shop around some more. She quickly learned that there were quite a few hard money lenders, each with an appetite for different kinds of risk. She discovered that hard money lenders were willing to take more risk than conventional financial institutions, but they usually traded that risk for a higher yield, higher up-front costs, and shorter loan terms.

After researching five hard money lenders, Marta felt she had learned enough about the industry norms to choose a lender. She picked the one that gave her the best deal and signed the paperwork to receive the money. As soon as she completed installing the new roof on her apartment building, refinanced with a conventional loan, paid back the hard money lender and breathed a huge sigh of relief.

Lessons _____

1. It's not unusual to hit a cash shortfall as you race along to hit your investment goals. A hard money lender can help you out of a pinch.

2. Always keep cash reserves, and prepare annual budgets.

3. Take the time to vet the lenders so that you can get the best terms for your project.

4. It's always easier to pay for renovations with your own money. Try to be realistic about the risks you're taking on with a property and budget accordingly, so you don't find yourself needing a hard money lender in the first place.

PART III:

OPERATIONS

15 THE NIGHTMARE AT THE BLACK CLOUD APARTMENTS

Name: Dolly

Property Type: Apartments

Famous Last Words: "The property looks reasonable, so the staff must be doing a good job. There's no need to double-check."

D olly had recently purchased a fifty-unit apartment complex called the Black Cloud Apartments. The location was great, most of the units were rented, and the closing took place on a cloudless sunny day. A good omen, Dolly thought. Because the previous owners had been using an on-site manager instead of a property management company, Dolly continued with this arrangement. This was where her problems began and led to the worst week Dolly could imagine. Let's start with day one.

Day One

It was the first of the month, and Martina, the on-site manager, was out collecting rents. Records showed that there were forty-seven occupied units and three vacant units. Martina went from door to door to collect the rents. Most tenants paid, but a few had to wait for their paychecks to clear. Martina said that if their rent was late, they needed to pay her an additional $50 late fee. The tenants understood there was a late fee, but what they didn't remember was that their rental agreements called for only a $25 late fee.

Martina had decided to create some additional income for herself. Averaging ten units late every month, Martina could make an extra $250.

She then visited the equipment storage room and checked in with the homeless man who camped there every night. "Hi, Rufus," she called. "Got your rent?" He handed over $100. Martina was letting him sleep in the storage room and wash up in the laundry room.

At ten a.m. a young Latino couple with one child showed up to rent a two-bedroom unit. Martina rented only to Russian immigrants so that she could control the property and ensure her cut of the rent. These applicants were employed, earned enough money, and had good references, clean credit, and no criminal records, but Martina told them there were no vacant units. Disappointed, the couple left the property.

An hour later, an elderly gay couple showed up to rent an apartment. Again, Martina said nothing was available.

Finally, close to the end of the day, a Russian family showed up. Martina invited them in for coffee and cake and told them about the special deal she had for them—which involved paying their rent plus a little more for her party fund. She didn't bother with any background checks even though the father had a history of misdemeanors and was unemployed with no job prospects in sight. She just let them move in.

That night when Dolly checked in on rent and apartment applications, Martina told her that the rents had been deposited and that only one family had shown up that day to look at vacant units. "Maybe we'll have better luck tomorrow," Martina said.

Martina did have rental applications and screening criteria that stated that they were to meet all Fair Housing Act guidelines and that they did not discriminate on the basis of race, color, religion, sex, handicap, national origin, familial or marital status, sexual orientation, or source of income. But of course, she ignored the information. She was the property gatekeeper, and she liked it that way.

Day Two

Martina had a live-in boyfriend, Boris, who did some limited work at the property. That day was his day to clean the gutters. He got the old wooden ladder out of the shed and leaned it up against the two-story building. It barely reached to the lip of the gutter, but he was young, and nothing scared him. As Boris reached the top of the ladder, his foot slipped, and he almost fell off the ladder, but he caught himself and held on to the gutter. Suddenly, the gutter spikes pulled out, and he fell to the ground. His back was badly hurt. Martina discovered him five minutes later and called an ambulance to take him to the hospital. The ladder lay in pieces on the ground. Dolly had no record of Boris on the rental agreement nor any record of him as an employee. She did not intend to pay workers' compensation coverage for him. Unfortunately, Boris had no insurance to cover the medical expenses to fix his broken back.

Day Three

A child playing in one of the units accidentally knocked over a lit candle, and the carpet caught fire. The unit burned. Due to quick response by the fire department, only one unit was destroyed, but two others had extensive smoke damage. Fortunately, Dolly had just purchased a new fire policy with a $5,000 deductible, so she had coverage for most of the fire damage.

Day Four

It was eight in the morning, and Dolly answered a knock on her door at home. A process server delivered a lawsuit notice from Boris to cover his medical costs, pain, suffering, and wage losses for the rest of his natural life. Five minutes later, a different process server handed her a summons regarding her fair housing violations. Dolly had been aware of Boris's situation, but she was completely surprised by the fair housing violations. She sat down at her dining room table to rub her temples and try to wrap her mind about what was happening with her new investment. Before she could even pull the papers out of the manila envelopes, Martina called to tell Dolly that she was quitting.

Dolly pulled herself together and went to inspect the property, review the fire situation, and visit with the tenants. She found utter chaos. Most of the tenants had maintenance issues that they said they had reported weeks prior. She finally sorted through them and headed to the maintenance closet for spare parts, where she discovered Rufus sleeping. When she asked him what he was doing, he told her he had paid his rent and to leave him alone. Dumbfounded and aware the insurance adjuster would be arriving any minute to inspect the apartments adjoining the fire damage, she said she'd be back and shut the door.

When Dolly and the insurance adjuster inspected the apartments, they found that none of the units had smoke detectors. That's odd, Dolly thought. She remembered that the smoke detectors had all been in the units during the inspection for the sale a week before, but it appeared Martina had collected them because none of the tenants had paid her a smoke detector fee. The fire marshal who was on site inspecting the fire damage joined them for the unit-by-unit inspections. As soon as it became obvious that there were no smoke detectors the fire marshal red tagged the property, and the insurance company pulled its coverage.

Dolly managed to remain composed until she got home, but there she crumbled onto the couch and broke down. How was it that everything could go wrong at once? She'd been so careful to do her due diligence on the property, coding, zoning, permits, and tenants that the operations should have been running smoothly. The only thing she'd not paid extensive attention to was Martina, but that was just one variable.

Day Five

First thing in the morning, Dolly called her attorney. She had several problems including displaced tenants, burned units, and two lawsuits on her hands. Furthermore, she had not yet registered the property as a limited liability company (LLC), so all her personal assets were at risk if the lawsuits did not go in her favor.

What had seemed like a great investment had turned into a nightmare.

Clearly Dolly should've inspected Martina's work before keeping her as the property manager, and the whole property would have done better with the help of a professional property management company. But she couldn't go back now. It was time to come up with a plan to fix all the damage.

One Month Later

Dolly found a property management company who helped her obtain temporary insurance. While the fire and smoke-damaged units were being fixed, the property manager started re-renting the other units and also put Rufus in touch with a housing transition project to help him get on his feet and out of the storage room. With the help of her attorney, Dolly formed a single-entity LLC, where she placed her property and settled the lawsuits. She renamed the property Happiness Hill Apartments to try to dispel the black-cloud image.

This scenario can happen to any owner of investment property. As part of the purchase of investment real estate, you need to ensure that policies are in place to prevent:

- Fair housing discrimination
- Manager theft
- Poor on site manager choices
- Lack of essential services (i.e., smoke detectors)
- Worker accident lawsuits

Protect yourself and your assets by using a single entity LLC. Consult your attorney, CPA, and property manager prior to closing a sale.

Lessons _____

1. Get professional help if you do not know what you are doing.

2. Don't be lazy with any details. Just because you've been diligent with 99 percent of the details, doesn't mean you're in the clear yet. That one percent could be the difference between a successful investment and a total failure.

16 METH LAB BLUES: CLEANING UP THE MESS

Investor Profile

Name: Darcy

Property Type: House

Famous Last Words: "If the rent checks are coming in, I have nothing to worry about. My tenants are perfect!"

D
arcy owned a small rental house in an Oregon suburb. She had inherited the house from her parents and had successfully been renting it out for twenty years. Usually the previous tenant would find a new tenant, so the house was almost never vacant.

Rent came in like clockwork, and the tenants never called her for repairs. As a matter of fact, it had been three years since she'd even stopped by the property for a visual inspection. Her current tenant was the daughter of a friend and was working at the local motel as a housekeeper.

An Unexpected Call

One Friday morning as Darcy was reading her newspaper, her telephone rang. It was the sheriff's office asking her to come to her rental property immediately.

What she saw when she arrived astonished her. The sheriff had just raised her house and arrested her tenant and the tenant's boyfriend. The investigators were wearing special suits with oxygen tanks on their backs. They looked like they were about to head into space.

Darcy approached the sergeant at the scene. "Can you tell me what's going on?"

Sergeant Underhill introduced himself and said, "We just arrested your tenants for manufacturing methamphetamine."

Darcy was shocked. Her house? Her tenant?

Sergeant Underhill then explained to her that he had called the county meth lab team to examine the house. She could have her house back when they had completed their evidence search, but tenants could not live in it until she had gone through the correct procedures to clean the house. The sergeant directed her to the state Department of Health website and gave her the name of an individual who could give her advice regarding the meth lab cleanup. He cautioned her that she should contact her attorney regarding how to evict the tenants. The sergeant estimated cleanup costs of approximately $12,000 but recommended Darcy get bids since prices varied among vendors.

Darcy left the scene totally dazed. What had she done wrong, and what was she going to do now?

Preventative Measures

As Darcy consulted with friends who also had rental properties, she realized she could've avoided this situation. Their advice included:

- Screen your tenants more carefully. Don't let anyone move in without a background check.
- Be aware of who lives at a property. Darcy should have known that the boyfriend had moved in, and then through the screening, she would have learned about his history of drug abuse and manufacturing.
- Inspect the property regularly, once a year at minimum. If the tenants refused to let her inspect the property, she would've had cause for concern and a motivation to evict them.

If Darcy had been regularly inspecting the house, she could've been looking for the following methamphetamine clues:

- Property condition: Yellow or red stains on countertops, carpets, or linoleum; windows blacked out or covered with foil
- Smell: Strong odors of cat urine, ether, ammonia, vinegar, or solvents
- Tenant behavior: Acting very high strung, talking very fast, wanting the landlord in and out of the unit or not there at all, accepting frequent visitors at all hours of the day and night
- Other evidence: Blister packs of ephedrine, cylinders, anhydrous ammonia, hydrochloric acid, empty solvent containers, mason jars, plastic tubing, rock salt, hydrogen peroxide, lithium batteries, or coffee filters with red stains

Then if any of these clues were evident, Darcy could have contacted the sheriff (or police), the state health department, or an industrial hygienist to confirm her suspicions. Tests usually take a week and can cost $500 or more, depending on the size of the property and/or the number of rooms, but that would have been better than the thousands Darcy now had to pay in cleaning and repairs, not to mention legal fees. If methamphetamine production was confirmed, Darcy should have asked the tenants to move out. Then she could have begun the cleanup process.

Cleanup

Even though Darcy now knew how to prevent this situation from happening again, she still had the current meth lab problem on her hands. Upon advice from the state health department and cleanup consultant, she hired a specialized vendor to clean up the house. She did not hire her handyman or cleaning crew to do the cleanup because she'd learned that methamphetamine and the products used during its manufacture are dangerous if inhaled or touched. Darcy didn't want to incur any liability or chance of being sued by her regular contractors, nor did she want to have the liability of being sued by future tenants if the property wasn't properly cleaned.

The cleanup crew had to take many steps to thoroughly clean the inside and outside of the rental house, including:

1. Air out the building.
2. Remove contaminated materials (carpets, carpet pads, linoleum, drapes and blinds, air filters, refrigerator, range, water heater, all tenant clothing and furniture) to a site that accepts contaminated product. All people who remove these items need to be specially trained and certified.
3. Clean extensively with bleach and other cleaners. Replace surfaces where the cooking occurred.
4. Replace furnaces and heaters or clean throughout all the ductwork.
5. Replace sinks, toilets, and other accessible plumbing because meth residue is often deposited down drains.
6. Clean, seal, and repaint the walls, ceilings, floors, and closets.
7. Clean windowpanes and tracks. If the unit is badly damaged, replace all the windows. Repaint doors on both sides and wash all door hardware.
8. Check if there is methamphetamine debris in the yard and properly dispose of the contaminated materials.

When Darcy talked to the state health department and did more research online, she learned that she was lucky—some property owners are faced with such high cleanup costs it's less expensive to just demolish the building. Even in this case, the materials would still need to be hauled to a special facility for disposal.

End in Sight

It took two weeks for the cleanup to be finished, and Darcy still had a few more tasks to tackle.

First, she hired an industrial hygienist to test and certify that the meth residue was totally cleaned up. The health department had told her that Oregon required a certificate of fitness (sometimes called an occupancy permit) that confirmed that the space was safe for a tenant to move back in or for the property to be re-rented after the cleanup was completed.

Next, Darcy tried to recover costs from the tenant. The tenant was in jail, but her father had cosigned on the lease, and as a result Darcy was able to recover 100 percent of the cleanup costs.

Still, the effects would be hard on Darcy for a while. Just the weekend before, she'd sat at her breakfast table to read the paper. Splashed on the front page was "Methamphetamine Raid" and a picture of Darcy's house surrounded by police. She cringed inside. It would take months or more before the community would forget about the raid on Darcy's property and trusted her as a landlord again. She should've inspected the property regularly, screened her tenants more carefully, and been a more hands-on landlord. It was a lesson learned the hard way.

Lessons

1. It does not matter if you know the tenants or their family— screen them carefully.

2. At the very least, drive by the property every so often to make sure nothing looks off and there aren't more tenants than are on the lease. And, inspect the property inside and out at least once a year.

17 NEVER RENT TO YOUR FRIENDS...OR THEIR KIDS

Investor Profile

Name: Ken
Property Type: Apartments
Famous Last Words: "Sure, I can do a favor for an old friend."

K en's friend Finley called him up and asked him to rent an apartment unit to his daughter, Stephanie. Ken and Finley had been golf buddies for twenty-five years, and Ken had no qualms about renting to Finley's family.

"Can you make an exception to your standard practices and not screen her, though?" Finley asked.

Ken hesitated. He'd been in the business for fifteen years by that point, and he'd never made an exception to this rule. He even had the following detailed rental criteria posted on his website:

Applying tenants must supply the following information with their rental application:

- A complete application for each adult eighteen or older (unfavorable information for any individual applicant may result in denial of all applications for that group)

- A three-year residency history including the names, addresses, and phone numbers of previous landlords. A three-year employment history including the names, addresses, and phone numbers of previous employers
- Verifiable gross monthly income that is three times the amount of rent (Verifiable income may mean, but is not limited to, salaried work with paystubs, self-employment with tax return, alimony/child support, trust accounts, Social Security, grants, or student loans.)
- If income is not verifiable, a current bank statement with a balance of five times the rent
- Two pieces of identification, one from each group below:
  Group A: Passport (foreign or US), US driver's license, or US state-issued ID card
  Group B: Social Security card, US birth certificate, Resident Alien card, work visa, or student visa
- Maximum occupancy of no more than two people per bedroom

Tenants may be asked to pay a higher deposit (up to twice the rent) if the following circumstances apply:

- No credit or poor credit (including slow pay or discharged bankruptcy more than one year ago)
- No landlord references (roommate and family references are not enough)
- Less than one year of rental history

Tenants will be denied and will forfeit their application fee if the following circumstances are true:

- Incomplete or misrepresentation of any information on the application
- Insufficient income
- Past eviction judgments
- Past felony charges and/or convictions, or three or more misdemeanor charges
- Discharged bankruptcy within the last twelve months or any open bankruptcy

- Negative landlord reference including: money owed to a prior landlord, three violation notices issued in a one-year period (such as seventy-two-hour notice, insufficient funds, noise or disturbance, or unauthorized pets or occupants), excessive damage upon move- out, or if a landlord refuses to give a reference

We accept the first qualified applicant.

Hearing Ken hesitate, Finley filled in, "She's just new to this whole renting business, and it intimidates her. I'll cosign, and you know I'm good for the money."

That was true—Ken did know Finley was good for the money. "You'll pay the deposit too?"

"Of course."

Before long, Finley was having furniture moved into the apartment, making it move-in ready for his daughter, but Ken's on-site manager noticed the unit still seemed vacant for the first six months. If he'd rented it to anyone other than Finley, he would've been worried. But because it was his friend, he pushed the matter to the back of his mind. Finally, Ken heard that Stephanie had moved in—with her cat.

For that, he had to call Finley.

"Oh, I'm sorry I forgot to mention that," Finley said. "How much do I owe you for a deposit?" With that, the issue was closed, and Ken went on to other business again.

Things went well for a while. Then Stephanie's boyfriend showed up, and soon the drama started. It seemed minor enough—just some noise complaints from the neighbors that Ken's on-site manager took care of—until Ken got a call from a police sergeant.

"Could you come down to the apartment complex? We're evacuating the tenants and planning a full-scale assault on one of the units."

Ken raced his car to the complex. Sure enough, there were four police cruisers and an armored personnel carrier in front of the building, all facing the apartment where Stephanie lived. But Ken was too late to try to coax her out—the police had already lobbed tear gas into the apartment. Damage was visible even from the street—shattered windows, broken siding—and Ken wondered what the inside would be like.

The police ran inside and came out with a man, probably Stephanie's boyfriend, but not Stephanie. Once the man was loaded into a cruiser, Ken demanded to have more information. "What's the meaning of this? Did you find what you were looking for? What about the damage to my property?"

"I understand you're upset, sir," the officer tried to calm him. "This man is arrested with charges of methamphetamine abuse and murder." He looked grim. "That's dangerous stuff, meth."

"What about my tenant? Was she involved?"

The officer explained that although Stephanie had quite a criminal history, they had no open warrants for her at the time. "It'd probably be a good idea to keep an eye on her, though."

Ken asked Stephanie to move out claiming the unit was not habitable. As Ken and his staff toured the apartment to assess the damage, Ken had a hard time breathing and knew he'd have to hire a professional clean- up crew to get the tear gas residue out of the ventilation system, walls, and carpets. Ken also smelled cat urine. *I should've asked Finley for a bigger pet deposit,* he thought. When he walked into the kitchen and saw stains on the countertops, though, it dawned on him that the cat urine smell wasn't from the cat—Stephanie and her boyfriend had been cooking meth.

Ken hired experts to clean the unit up as well as an industrial hygiene company to test and confirm the apartment was safe for the next tenant. It took two months to clean up before new tenants could move in. Fortunately for Ken, Finley had agreed to pay all costs of his daughter's tenancy. Unfortunately for Ken, his friend's family was going through a rough time.

"I'm sorry about your daughter," he told Finley, not sure how much he would be seeing his friend for a while.

The Good News

The good news was that Ken learned his lesson. From then on, he screened all tenants before they could be approved to move in. It was a painful and costly lesson, but an important one—not just for the financial success of his business but also to ensure a safe community for his tenants to live in.

Lessons _____

1. Screen everyone. And if they have a roommate or significant other move in, insist on screening them too.

2. Stick to your ethics even when a friend is asking for a favor. It's much easier to say, "I'm sorry, but we have to put everyone through the formal application process," than it is to lose thousands of dollars and put that strain on your friendship.

18 MAKE MONEY WITH QUICK TENANT TURNS

Investor Profile

Name: Taylor
Property Type: Apartments
Famous Last Words: "Apartments basically fill themselves. There's not really any work that goes into it."

Taylor was just out of high school and excited to have her first job as an assistant property manager. She would be working under Joyce, the on-site manager at the Green Pineapple Apartments in Oregon City, Oregon. Since all the units looked like they were full, Taylor thought it would be an easy job mainly consisting of watching soap operas in the complex office and maybe answering the phone occasionally. Even if people were to move out, Taylor figured all she'd have to do was put up a Craigslist posting to find more tenants.

When she went to Joyce's office to check in on her first day of work, the tidy desk and the shining plaques on the wall let Taylor know that she might be in for a surprise. *Oh well*, she thought. *It can be boring to sit around all day.*

When Joyce looked up and said, "Oh good, you're here. We have so much to do," Taylor decided she'd learn all she could about property management from this woman.

The first thing Joyce told Taylor was that their mission was to turn vacant units in less than a week between move-out and new tenant move-in. "Every day a unit goes unrented," Joyce emphasized, "is a day the company loses money." To manage that quick turnaround, they had to be extremely well organized.

The Week Before

"The Johnsons are moving out in one week," Joyce told Taylor. "We'll meet with Mrs. Johnson today to cover everything she needs to know for that." Taylor was surprised. She and her family had lived in apartments for years and had moved several times, and she didn't remember there ever being open communication with the landlord before they moved out.

Joyce, Taylor, and the maintenance supervisor headed to the Johnsons' apartment to gauge the repairs they needed to address for move-out. They checked each room, turning on the heaters and appliances to make sure they were in working order. They inspected the bathrooms and kitchen to make sure the spigots didn't leak, and the tubs, sinks, and toilets drained properly. From carpeting to windows, and sheetrock to molding, they inspected it all.

"I don't see any major damage, Mrs. Johnson," Joyce said. "Just please be sure to putty the holes in the walls as you take your pictures down, and we should be able to start the normal maintenance and cleaning process right away, which means you shouldn't lose any of your deposit." She handed the tenant a checklist of things to do before move-out, and it included names and contact information of a carpet-cleaning company, a handyman, a moving company, places to get used moving boxes, U-Haul locations, and the local Goodwill, as well as companies that would pick up slightly damaged furniture or unwanted clothing.

Finally, Joyce used the opportunity to get the tenant's forwarding address, so the security deposit could be mailed as quickly as possible.

As they headed back to the office, Joyce explained to Taylor, "A lot of property managers don't meet with tenants before move-out, but we do.

That way, if there's a significant amount of tenant-caused damage or even if it's just the usual wear and tear, the tenants know before they move out and can do their own repairs if they want to help mitigate the damages."

Opening the door, she added, "It saves us time too, since we can plan ahead for whatever repairs might need to happen." Then she called the painting and cleaning crews to give them a heads-up about the upcoming move-out.

Move-Out Day

Taylor could see that Joyce was a pro, and that made dealing with tenant move-outs straightforward. On move-out day, she and Taylor met the Johnsons and completed the final walk-through.

"This family has been in the unit for five years," Joyce told Taylor, "so the carpet will need to be replaced." She made a note on her paperwork and then handed the clipboard to Taylor. "Here, why don't you fill it in the rest of the way? We need to schedule blind removal too."

Taylor made a note.

"Luckily there are no fleas," Joyce went on, "or else we'd need to schedule an extra day for a flea bomb."

Taylor learned that after the tenant moved out, the turn schedule looked something like this:

Days 1–3: General maintenance

Day 4: Cleaning and painting

Day 5: Carpet replacement or cleaning, lock changes

Over the next few days, Joyce taught Taylor how to replace light bulbs and globes, range drip pans, and broken switch and outlet plates. "And always test the smoke detectors," she said. "It's the law."

When Joyce explained that little things like putting out a new welcome mat and repainting the front door and its trim helped new tenants feel at home, Taylor wished her family rented from Joyce. The front of their apartment had looked so dingy when they first moved in. To give the unit a new-home feel, Joyce installed a new bathroom sink and baseboard heater too.

Finding the New Tenant

Ten days before the tenant had moved out, Joyce had already begun searching for a new tenant. She placed advertising on Craigslist, called prospects on her waiting list, and made sure the website had the correct information. She had already coordinated with her district manager at the central office regarding the rental rate and completed her quarterly rental surveys. She explained all this to Taylor and told her that she'd take the lead on these tasks with the next move-out.

"Based on our research," Joyce said, "we can raise the rent by $50 per month over the previous rent. We have to make sure that everywhere we post the vacancy has the correct new rent."

Taylor had noticed the phone was ringing for showings since she first walked into the office, but she had assumed it was for other vacant units. Now she realized that because Joyce was so good at planning ahead, people were calling about this unit.

"The Johnsons are nice and allowed us to take some tours through before move-out," Joyce said.

Then Taylor noticed the stack of applications on Joyce's desk. "Those are for the Johnson's unit already, aren't they?"

Joyce smiled. "You catch on quick."

Move-In Day

As day six dawned, Joyce and Taylor were ready, and so was the newly approved tenant. Denny arrived at nine to fill out the rental agreement and collect keys to the newly rekeyed apartment. The three of them walked through the unit and completed a move-in inspection. Joyce had Taylor take pictures of the unit with the office's iPad to include in the unit file with the inspection notes. They then signed the rental agreement, and the new tenant moved in right on schedule.

Everyone was happy. Taylor was learning a lot at her new job, and she liked that her supervisor was well organized. She learned a process that was well orchestrated and executed, and she could see how important it was for the success of the business, as it resulted in an improved unit with increased rent. Joyce had hit her turn goal and only lost five days of rent. The landlord thought Joyce was a superstar—and she was.

Lessons _____

1. Keeping an apartment complex full all the time takes a lot of planning.

2. When you plan the whole move-out process with the tenants as well as the maintenance and cleaning crews, people appreciate the extra communication.

3. Planning the turnaround even before move-out helps you get new tenants in faster, which leads to a more successful business.

19 SURVEY YOUR TENANTS: THEIR SATISFACTION IS MONEY IN YOUR POCKET

Investor Profile

Name: Gloria
Property Type: Apartments
Famous Last Words: "I already know my property and staff are amazing. Still, it wouldn't hurt to ask the tenants."

Gloria woke up early, fully invigorated and ready to do her annual quality control check-in. Her goal for the day was to read tenant surveys for all the properties she owned—more than two hundred units. This was no small project, but Gloria was determined to do a good job. She knew that the happier her tenants were, the longer they would stay—and the longer they stayed, the more money she would make.

The Costs of Tenant Turnover

Early in Gloria's career she had been a property manager—before she started buying her own properties—her supervisor had taught her to pay attention to what tenants wanted and that if she kept them happy, it would pay off.

"Think of it this way," he said. "Every tenant turnover result's in cleaning and painting expenses, maintenance expenses, and wear and tear on the hallways, stairwells, and elevators as tenants move in and out. Just look outside and see how many carports, downspouts, and gutters have been damaged by moving trucks." He pointed. "Consider the advertising expenses, the leasing expenses, the hassle of showing units and screening new tenants."

Gloria understood that all these expenses added together were significant, so if she could reduce the number of tenants vacating each month, she'd reduce her expenses and increase her return on investment.

After nearly ten years in the business, Gloria knew that, as a general industry-wide rule, most apartment tenancies lasted twelve to sixteen months, or as a general average, 50 percent of the units turned or became vacant every year. Gloria's numbers were slightly better than that, but she'd done this survey to see how she could improve it even more. *Just think of the savings if only a third of my tenants moved instead of almost half,* she pondered.

The Survey

Let's face it: Gloria couldn't be at her properties twenty-four hours a day, seven days a week. Things would happen that she wasn't aware of—the trash hauler could carelessly leave the dumpster or trash cans blocking a car, the person she'd hired to answer the phones could have a grumpy tone, the maintenance worker could forget to wipe his feet. While not all these things were necessarily immediately damaging, they could contribute to tenants' general dissatisfaction, and Gloria did not want that. By surveying them, Gloria gave her tenants an opportunity to share their thoughts about issues they may have been too busy or too afraid to tell her or her on-site managers face-to-face.

Over the years, Gloria had gotten feedback from her tenants in various ways:

1. She randomly asked tenants when she visited her properties and saw them outside or in the offices.
2. She sent them written surveys with stamped self-addressed envelopes to be returned to her.

3. She surveyed them electronically via a service like SurveyMonkey, Zoomerang, SurveyGizmo, Polldaddy, or Constant Contact.
4. She always kept a spot on her property websites where tenants could leave comments.

Since online survey technology had become so easy to use by this point, that was mainly what Gloria used for her intermittent full-tenant surveys, although she still collected feedback by chatting with tenants and collecting comments on the website.

Her surveys included questions like the following:

- Is your on-site manager available during posted hours?
- Are the posted office hours convenient for you?
- Is the office staff courteous and helpful?
- Are you satisfied with the maintenance work completed at your home/apartment?
- Does the maintenance team pick up after itself once the maintenance is completed?
- Are the common areas (laundry room, yard, parking area) kept clean and tidy?
- How would you rate the condition of your unit at move-in?
- If you are not happy, what are your major concerns?
- Do you feel your problems are resolved promptly?
- Would you rent from us again?
- Are you satisfied with the accounting?
- Are there other concerns that we should be aware of?
- Are you interested in participating in on-site activities?

Gloria was also curious about whether the move-in fees and rents the tenants paid on move-in matched the written records. She'd heard about dishonest property managers who charged additional fees or deposits (like parking fees, reservation deposits, extra key fees, or transfer fees) and pocketed the extra money, so she always polled new tenants a month after move-in and included questions about what they'd paid when they executed the rental agreements and paid their first month's rents, fees, and deposits.

Gloria wanted to personally review all the tenant surveys to make sure she and her managers were giving her tenants exemplary service. Most importantly, she wanted to personally respond to her tenants with a letter and then make improvements to her properties and policies. As legitimate problems were uncovered, she always fixed them. She knew that if she did not respond to her tenants and resolve the issues, then no one would answer the next survey and her turnover rate was likely to go up instead of down.

Survey Results

Gloria knew that not all her tenants would return her surveys. As much as she would've loved a 100 percent return rate, it was more realistic to anticipate that 10 to 30 percent of her tenants would respond. Survey respondents tended to fall into two extremes: those who were extremely happy and impressed, and those who were extremely unhappy and disappointed. The middle, silent majority were often too busy or neutral to take the time to respond. To entice as many people as possible to respond, Gloria kept the survey short—possible to complete in just a couple of minutes—and offered a coupon for a free pizza to tenants who completed the survey.

Gloria also made sure tenants knew their surveys were kept private— she wouldn't share them with other tenants or people outside her company— but they were not anonymous. She set up the online surveys to let her identify the tenants responding so she could sort out the problems at their units, which might include maintenance concerns, issues with other tenants, or problems with the on-site manager. She typically surveyed annually and compared her results to the previous couple of years to confirm that the results were improving.

While all the information on the survey was critical, the most important question, in her opinion, was the one that asked, "Would you rent from us again?" This gave her insight into tenant satisfaction with the property, the maintenance staff, and the on-site manager. Her goal was that 85 percent of the tenants who responded were happy living at the property. She felt that if she reached that number, she was on the right track.

Once Gloria had her cup of coffee flavored with her favorite vanilla syrup, she sat down at the computer and clicked into the survey. The program first told her that of her more than two hundred units, sixty-three had responded. Not too bad. Then she had the program run a satisfaction report related to the question about whether people would rent from her again: 87 percent said yes. Excellent!

Feeling buoyed by this good news, Gloria decided it was time to look at the rest of the questions. She had the program run a report that showed the percentage of satisfaction for each question the tenants responded to. She quickly saw that the lowest-scoring question was "Is the office staff courteous and helpful?" *Uh-oh*, she thought. She clicked through to see that 45 percent of responders rated the office staff at one of her properties as poor on the service scale. She clicked on the comments portion of the survey, thinking people might have elaborated there, but not many did. She'd have to do some follow-up work.

Gloria composed an email to each tenant who scored the office service as poor. First, she thanked them for completing the survey and then mentioned that she had a few follow-up questions based on their responses. She wanted to know if the tenants only got voicemail and never a human being on the phone, if they had to call numerous times before getting a response, or if they were expected to wait an extended period of time for a resolution to their problems. She also knew that general demeanor could mean a lot when it came to customer service satisfaction, so she added a question about whether the staff was friendly. She asked people to respond with their feedback within four days, so she'd have time to integrate the new information with the rest of the survey results before she had to act. Again, not everyone responded, but enough people wrote back that Gloria understood that her office staff was generally slow to respond and brusque when they did, bordering on rude. Nobody had any major problems to report, just general dissatisfaction.

That's something I can work with, Gloria thought. She would simply schedule a mandatory training for the office staff where she'd cover customer service guidelines such as answering the phone by the second ring, smiling when talking with customers, and submitting maintenance requests right away. Thinking back to her first supervisor whom she'd learned so much from, Gloria remembered the lesson, "No matter what's going on in your life outside of work, when you get here, you leave your problems at the door." Her supervisor had said, "If you create that separation, you can always provide excellent customer service. It helps in your personal life, too, when you have bad days at work—and no matter how wonderful your job is, those will come up sometimes." After Gloria scheduled the training session with her staff, she also made a note on her calendar to survey the dissatisfied tenants again in two months. Surely, they'd all see an improvement.

Gloria explored the other results of the survey, took care of any issues she noticed, and wrote to each respondent with a personalized note and a coupon for free pizza. A nice side benefit, she noticed, was that when people had the opportunity to voice their concerns in the survey and she could fix them, they were less likely to write their negative feedback on online venues like Yelp, Google, or Citysearch and were even more likely to post positive reviews in such places, boosting her properties' internet reputation.

She was also realistic regarding the results, since she knew that the middle, silent majority were often too busy or neutral to take the time to respond. She worked hard to get a percentage of those tenants to respond. At the end of the day, she was also able to discover that at one of her properties, the on-site maintenance technician was overwhelmed and could not catch up. At another property she discovered that the on-site manager was charging fees that went into his own pocket, and finally she discovered why her third property was renting so slowly: the manager had two other jobs and was never on-site to show units. Once again, the annual tenant survey had paid off, and Gloria was very pleased with herself.

Lessons _____

1. There is always room to improve your property and the management of the property. Tenant surveys help you see where to focus your efforts.

2. Be prepared to receive both good and bad news, and always respond to issues that need improvement. If you don't, your tenant satisfaction will drop rapidly.

3. The higher the tenant satisfaction, the longer tenants will stay, and even when they do move, their word-of-mouth advertising will fill your units right up again.

20 RELIABLE VENDORS = HAPPY OWNERS

Investor Profile

Names: Marcel and Maxine

Property Type: Apartments/Houses/Commercial Building

Famous Last Words: "We can do all of the maintenance ourselves. No problem!"

Marcel loved real estate. He owned five houses and a commercial building. He was proud that he did all the maintenance himself since he was trained as a plumber, an electrician, and a carpenter. Hands-on tasks were his strength. So, whenever he bought a property, he budgeted nothing for maintenance labor costs because he was going to repair it all himself.

Maxine was a great painter and thought she could paint and make repairs to a property herself. She owned a twenty-unit apartment property in a great part of town. It had 12 studios and 8 one-bedroom apartments, and the repairs were not extensive—yet.

Investors Meet

Marcel and Maxine were both single. They met at a landlord association meeting and realized they had a lot in common. Being a

109

landlord, of course, was one of their shared passions. They had built their own individual real estate empires, so they could fund their retirement.

They also liked architecture and traveling. Once they met, they were inseparable. They spent every spare moment together outside of work— and a lot during work too. They started trading services: he maintained her units, and she painted his. It seemed like a great match.

But the tenants were not very happy. The repairs were slipshod and inexpensively done, so the tenants did not stay very long. Marcel and Maxine, however, thought they were doing fine.

Catastrophe Hits

Reality set in when the roof started leaking on Maxine's apartments and Marcel claimed he could fix it. He pulled out the big ladder and leaned it against the building, but as he got to the top, there was a big earthquake and Marcel's ladder tumbled to the ground, breaking his shoulder. He didn't have health insurance. The cost of his rehabilitation exceeded $25,000, and he didn't have that much cash readily available. The medical collection companies immediately recognized that he had real estate and put a lien on one of his houses. Beyond that, he couldn't do any of his repairs. Marcel was crushed.

Maxine did the best she could with the repairs to their properties, but she also wanted to save money to pay Marcel's medical bills. The stress was significant, and Maxine just wanted to run away. "Let's go on vacation from the tenants," she said to Marcel. However, there was no one to take care of the tenants because neither of them had backup vendors.

Marcel was the voice of reason. "We really need to find vendors to cover for us while we're gone."

Maxine winced; she hated wasting money, but she understood.

Finding Vendors

Marcel and Maxine started the process of finding vendors. They first made a list of the categories of maintenance and then sub-lists of service providers needed.

Tenant turnover:

1. Painter
2. General cleaner
3. Carpet cleaner
4. Blind and curtain cleaner

Normal maintenance:

- Roofer
- Locksmith
- Plumber
- Electrician
- Dry rot repair
- Rooter company
- Emergency response company for overflows and fires
- Flooring
- Pest control
- Appliance repair
- Heating Ventilation Air Conditioning (HVAC)

Long term:

- Property manager

Then they started asking their friends for recommendations for reliable and reasonable vendors and finally started trying them out. Both Marcel and Maxine were surprised how much more time they now had to spend together. Beyond that, the repairs looked so much more professional than they had before, and they didn't have to bother the tenants so much because the repairs were done right the first time.

So, they booked their trip to Costa Rica knowing their investments were in good hands.

Lessons _____

1. Insist that vendors are licensed and bonded and have the appropriate insurance for themselves and their employees.

2. Keep a list of professional maintenance vendors, even if you do repairs yourself. You are bound to need to hire someone at some point. You might even decide that life is easier when you hire out!

21 CHOOSING THE RIGHT VENDOR FOR YOUR PROPERTY

Investor Profile

Name: Jules
Property Type: Apartments/Houses/Retail Center
Famous Last Words: "I like to just hire the first vendor I call."

In six years as a property owner, Jules had been faced with numerous challenges with his vendors. One of his apartment properties had its own sewage pump because the sewer line at the property was located below the city's gravity-fed system. The sewage pump failed over a long weekend, so Jules called a plumbing contractor who wanted $5,000 to replace the sump pump. The cost for the pump was $1,000, so the labor charge alone was $4,000 for about five hours' worth of work. Jules was shocked, but he needed it replaced immediately, so he agreed. He later learned that this plumber earned a commission of 50 percent from the company he contracted through—no wonder he set his bid so high.

Another time, one of Jules's houses needed a new roof. A roofer installed it and included a ten-year warranty, but within a year, the new roof started leaking. When Jules tried to call him, the roofer had gone out of business, so the warranty was worthless.

A painter bid a strip-mall project and asked for half the money up front to cover painting expenses. After Jules paid the down payment, the painter ignored the project, took the money, and went on vacation. Jules sued that painter.

His most recent issue was when he hired a drain cleaning company to clear a drain line. Unfortunately, the blades on the drain cleaner destroyed the pipe. Was the pipe old? Or did the company destroy the pipe? Jules felt it was operator error since the property was only ten years old. He was still in the midst of trying to sue that vendor.

As an astute manager of real estate investments, Jules knew it was important to limit errors and improve operating returns. So far, though, the vendors he had hired had mostly just cost him a lot of money.

Specifications and Scope

From the drainage experience, Jules learned that he needed to improve the instructions he was giving vendors, no matter what he was hiring them for. He had a painting project coming up, so he started by learning everything he could about paint. He knew his properties needed the exteriors repainted every seven years. But he didn't know how to find a painter who would do a good job or how to define the specifications and scope of each job to help the painter do the job right. When Jules looked for answers online, he soon found himself overwhelmed.

So, he went to a paint supply store and asked questions. The saleslady was very understanding, and the first thing she did was give Jules a copy of the store's paint specifications worksheet to detail the work that needed to be completed at any property.

"It's easy," she said. "Fill this worksheet out, and just about any painter should have a firm grasp of what you need done."

Jules looked the worksheet over and agreed it seemed easy. It read:
Surfaces to Be Painted
In the following lists, indicate the specific materials of each interior and exterior surface—for example, brick, wood, plaster, metal, cement, render, and so on— and whether they are new or previously painted. The

material and condition of the surfaces will impact the level of preparation required, the sealing process required, and the number of finishing coats needed—and ultimately the final quality and cost.

Interior:

- Walls
- Ceilings
- Doors
- Windows
- Trims
- Floors

Exterior:

- Siding
- Roof
- Gutters/drain pipes
- Fence/gates
- Doors
- Windows
- Garage
- Deck/pathways

Preparation Required

Preparation is critical for long-lasting results.

- Re-puttying of window glazing
- Mold removal
- Washing/cleaning surfaces
- Dust, grease, or scale removal
- Rust removal
- Loose or flaking paint removal
- Hole, crack, or broken plaster patching
- Sanding
- Fitting removal
- Priming and sealing
- Window and door caulking
- Soffit and siding repairs

Selection of Painting Materials and Colors

Some surfaces and colors will require more coats than others. The more specific an owner can be about colors and materials, the more likely the painter will be able to achieve the desired outcome.

- Color palette
- Paint brand
- Gloss level
- Depth of paint application
- Surface priming
- Number of coats
- Paint samples

Method of Application

The best method of application will depend on the type of finish being applied, the desired results, the type of surface, and your budget.

- Brush
- Roller
- Spray
- Powder coating (for railings, doors, and playgrounds)

Site Preparation and Cleanup

Ensure that the quotes include information on protecting plants and landscaping as well as necessary tree and bush trimming to access paintable surfaces.

- Rubbish removal
- Paint disposal
- Splatter removal
- Landscape/outdoor furniture protection

Vendor name:

Bid:

Jules learned how important it was to communicate these specifications and the scope of the work up front. He also made a note to check in with the vendors often as they worked on the job to make sure they were completing the work in sync with the specifications and scope.

Then the clerk gave Jules a list of reputable licensed, bonded, and insured painters in the area.

"Thank you so much." He was relieved to have such solid guidance in hiring a good painter, and he set about collecting similar materials for roofers and plumbers too.

Building Referrals

The list of painters that the clerk gave Jules was a great start, but he still needed to build up his list of potential vendors in all service areas. He started by asking his friends and other property owners to recommend a few vendors. Whenever he worked with a vendor he liked, he also asked them if they could recommend vendors for noncompeting services. Then he joined his local rental owners' organization and found that the other members there were often quick to recommend their favorite vendors.

Building his lists by word-of-mouth recommendations seemed to be working well.

"Keep in mind, though," warned one of the property owners in the organization, "that some people make recommendations because the vendor gives them a referral kickback. Those aren't true recommendations, so always ask if someone is being paid to make a recommendation."

Jules thought he'd go one step further than the word-of-mouth recommendations and went online to build up his lists with vendors he found on DexKnows and Angie's List. He was shocked to learn that vendors on these sites could use tricks to be ranked at top of the list. Vendors on these sites were good marketers but not necessarily competent service providers.

Collecting Bids

Most property owners are driven by vendor pricing. Investors always want the least expensive price and the best value they can find, and Jules was no different. Unfortunately, low prices sometimes mean substandard work due to lack of licensing or insurance, a misunderstanding, or plain old inexperience.

By now, Jules had learned that it made sense to meet with at least three vendors and obtain three bids, at least on larger jobs.

"You'll probably end up with a list of your favorite vendors," one of the helpful sales clerks told him. "And for your small jobs here and there, there's probably no harm in just hiring your buddy who's done a good job for you before. For your big jobs, though, every single time, get at least three bids. Good vendors know it is just business, and you have to do what's best for your project, they all have references you can call.

Jules made specifications worksheets, like the painting one, for every type of vendor he might need, and he also had the great idea to provide each vendor with a sketch of the property layout along with the bid worksheet. With this, he could mark where he wanted the repairs to take place, and the vendors could mark the places where they expected to need extra prep or cleanup work.

More than the Bid

Over the course of the plumbing, painting, and roofing fiascos, Jules had learned that price was not the only thing to consider when choosing which vendor to hire. Other key factors included professionalism, recalls, cleanliness, response to emergency situations, and the fine print in every vendor's contract, specifically with an eye to liens and lien releases as well as quality and timeliness of the work.

To go along with his bid specifications worksheet and property sketch, Jules made his own worksheet to evaluate his interview with each vendor:

Professionalism

- Does the vendor care that the job is done in a professional manner?
- Will they do it right the first time, using products and parts that will last?
- Will they limit their work to authorized repairs?
- Is the staff well trained with the right skill set and tools?

- Will they issue a warranty or guarantee of more than thirty days?
- Do they have general liability and workers' compensation insurance?
- Do they have a contractor's license, and are they bonded?
- If they hire subcontractors to perform the job, who is responsible for liens and quality control?

Recalls

- Is the vendor willing to admit mistakes?
- Will they give a credit for mistakes made?
- If required, will they redo the job?

Cleanliness

- Will the job site be cleaned before they leave?
- Will they protect tenants' possessions?

The Fine Print

Does the fine print of the vendor's bid all make sense? Pay special attention to:

- The vendor's specific rules that the owner and the tenants are expected to comply with
- When the late payment fees kick in and at what rate they accrue
- Collection procedures if there is payment delay
- Mediation to solve disputes
- Lien releases for large jobs

Emergencies

- Is the vendor available twenty-four hours a day, 365 days a year?
- How much extra do they charge for emergency responses?

Now that Jules was collecting at least three bids on every big job, he was learning that this process of researching, interviewing, and considering bids was somewhat time consuming but well worth it. Now he could identify which vendors were knowledgeable about their services, understood what he needed to be done, and collected the best—which was not necessarily the cheapest—bid.

Lessons _____

1. It is your job to define the scope and specifications of the project to the vendors. Once you can do that clearly, you can expect high-quality work.

2. Build a list of potential vendors based on word-of-mouth recommendations from other property owners or people in the industry.

3. Get at least three bids on every big project. Consider cost, professionalism, and understanding of the scope of the project.

22 NOW THAT YOU OWN REAL ESTATE... KEEP YOUR EYE ON IT

Investor Profile

Name: Matthew
Property Type: Retail/Warehouse
Famous Last Words: "I've inherited what?"

On a random Thursday morning, Matthew received a phone call from an attorney who claimed that he had inherited some real estate investments from his uncle. Matthew was the last remaining heir of the McCoen dynasty and needed to travel to New Jersey to meet with the attorney. Matthew was Oregon born and bred, so he fit in well in the Northwest. He loved the outdoors and the organic foods that farmers grew in the area. He was a free spirit of sorts, and his home was the only real estate he owned. The whole concept of being involved with real estate investments boggled his mind. On the other hand, Matthew had never shied away from a new challenge, so he flew to New Jersey.

Meeting the Attorney

Attorney Lily Suessman explained to Matthew, that his uncle had three properties that he was going to inherit. All the buildings were in

Union County, New Jersey.

Lily suggested that they look at all the properties. When she excused herself to change from her business attire to jeans and a T-shirt and hiking boots, Matthew thought it was odd but said nothing. They headed to the properties in her SUV.

Inspecting the Properties

The first property was a convenience store located at a great intersection near the Newark airport, and the other two were warehouses that Matthew's uncle had used in his businesses.

The convenience store was rented, but the property needed a paint job, landscaping, and a new roof. The lease for this 2,500-square-foot property with a large parking lot was just $500 a month—not a good return on investment.

As they drove up to the warehouses, Lily said, "Now you'll understand why I changed my clothes." The first one was overgrown with weeds; they had to take out a machete from the trunk of her car to cut their way into the property. It was a 10,000-square-foot warehouse that was filled, from stem to stern, with inventory left over from Matthew's uncle's business of distributing souvenirs and postcards all over the East Coast.

"So, I have a warehouse full of plastic Civil War toys, Liberty Bells, and Statues of Liberty," Matthew said. Clearly his uncle had been a collector. The other warehouse, which was located across the street, looked just as it had when Matthew's uncle closed his business. The wooden chairs and desks were in place where they had been when the employees left the building; the calendars still read 1992. This was a 5,000-square-foot brick building with plumbing and electrical that dated back seventy-five years. It, too, was filled with collectibles. Matthew was nonplussed.

Developing a Plan

He asked Lily, "Now what do I do?"

She laughed and replied, "Well, you're lucky. He left you some cash too, so you can decide whether you're going to keep the properties or sell them. If you want to sell, you can also decide if you're going to fix them up first or sell them in as-is condition."

Matthew realized his uncle hadn't paid attention to his real estate investments. He figured it must have been too much effort for him, and he wasn't sure if it was going to be too much effort for him too since he lived far away. But these seemed like good locations, and he remembered that his uncle had felt very strongly about not selling them. Lily seemed to sense Matthew's thoughts. "I'd be happy to help you develop a strategy to keep the properties and improve them."

Matthew smiled. "I'll need all the help you can give me."

They returned to her office and reviewed the lease for the convenience store. The lease had expired, and the tenant was there on a month-to-month basis and was interested in staying. They hired two brokers to assess the value of the property and share their opinions regarding the lease rate. The brokers suggested that the lease rate could exceed $3,000 a month and that Matthew would be able to make an additional $1,000 a month leasing exterior signage to Clear Channel. The tenants agreed to the rate as long as Matthew made repairs first. He did this and signed a ten-year lease with the tenant that included annual 3 percent increases.

Matthew and Lily also proceeded to empty out the warehouses and sell the entire inventory to the discount chain Big Lots. They then rewired and replumbed the two warehouses, seal-coated the parking lots, tuck-pointed the brick, and put a new roof on each building. The warehouses leased right away, both with ten-year leases.

The cash Matthew's uncle had left him wasn't quite enough to pay for all the repairs, though, so he had to place a loan on one of the buildings. This process took three months, so he didn't stay in New Jersey the whole time.

He did get the properties turned around, and he kept them. It cost over $500,000 to rehab the properties, but the final value of the estate after he made all the repairs was more than $2 million. So it was well worth the time and money invested.

Lessons _____

1. It can pay to invest in real estate, but don't ignore your investments. If you do, you—or your family—will have to invest even more to rehab them.

2. If you inherit property, consider all your options. It might be best to sell, but it could also be worth it to update and find tenants. A professional can help you decide what's best.

23 STAYING ON TRACK WITH MONTHLY FINANCIAL REPORTS

Investor Profile

Name: Rick
Property Type: Retail Center
Famous Last Words: "The bookkeeper does all of the reports. I don't need to see them."

R
ick owned Zonko Motorcycles, where he helped design specialty motorcycles one component at a time. As the business matured, he was able to afford a 10,000-square-foot retail neighborhood shopping center. He named it Molly's Corner after his wife. He put a Zonko dealership into one end of the building, taking up 2,000 square feet, and leased the rest to five other tenants on a triple net basis. He had a pizza parlor, a dentist, a boutique, an electronics store, and an ice-cream shop.

The Financial Tangle

Rick asked his bookkeeper, Sally, to keep track of the property's income and expenses. One spring day, five years after he had purchased the building, he received a letter in the mail from his bank, which had financed the purchase of the building.

Rick was late with his mortgage payment, and the bank was looking for his annual financial statements for the property. Rick checked with Sally, and she told him she hadn't prepared any financial statements for the property. Instead, she'd consolidated the property's income and expense numbers in the Zonko financial reports.

Rick pondered this for a minute and then instructed her to set up a file for the property itself.

Pandora's Box

As Rick instructed, Sally established financial statements for Molly's Corner. Rick looked them over but felt something was wrong—his losses on the property were significant, so he took them to his CPA, Tom, to review.

"Do these numbers look right to you?" Tom asked.

Rick shrugged. "That's why I thought you should look at them."

Tom then called Jeremy, a commercial property manager, for advice. The three of them set up a meeting to review the financials, and Jeremy asked Rick to bring copies of the leases. Jeremy had driven by the property before the meeting and had a pretty good handle on the location the property was in and the rents for the area.

The meeting was tense. Once they looked closer, they discovered that the Zonko store had never paid rent to Rick. Sally had not thought it necessary to mention it to Rick.

Upon review of the leases, Jeremy pointed out that the pizza parlor had never paid any increases in rent and that the dentist never paid any of the triple net (NNN) expenses. Rick was embarrassed—and it got worse. The ice-cream shop was leased to Rick's nephew, and he had never paid rent.

On the expense side, it seemed that Rick had huge outstanding payables. Taxes were delinquent, water bills had not been paid, and the mortgage was one month late. Tom had prepared Rick's taxes properly, but Rick had thought Sally was writing the checks. She wasn't always doing it.

The perspiration was building up on Rick's forehead. It seemed like every time he wrapped his head around one problem, three more cropped up. "What should I do?" Rick questioned.

Jeremy suggested, "First you need to pay the mortgage and the back taxes. Then you need to establish a routine of monthly financial reports for this property. It needs to stand on its own, separate from Zonko Motorcycles." Rick nodded. Breaking it down into steps seemed to help. He could do one thing at a time.

Jeremy went on. "I would encourage you to also keep track of the rents and receive a monthly rent-roll, expense register, and aging report. And it's a good idea to audit the tenant leases once a year. Those tenants who haven't paid rent need to pay or move out, including your Zonko dealership. Triple Net charges, need to be calculated, billed for, and collected from all tenants too." This was starting to feel like too much for Rick again, but then he saw that Jeremy was writing it all down. That helped.

As he handed Rick the list, Jeremy said, "Once you put in place all your controls and get monthly financial reports, I think you'll find that this property can be a moneymaker. But you've got to keep your eye on the financials."

After pausing for a moment, Jeremy added, "When I drove by Molly's Corner, I noticed some maintenance issues. You'll want to keep an eye on maintenance to make sure the property stays in tip-top shape and keeps its value."

Rick was grateful for the advice. He promptly fired Sally and transferred his bookkeeping to Tom's firm, emphasizing the need for two separate monthly financial reports—Zonko Motorcycles and Molly's Corner.

At home that night, Rick told Molly, "I guess owning property isn't like putting money into a savings account, where you can sort of forget about it. I've learned that you have to be involved in the property and pay attention to it; otherwise, you lose control and revenues." Molly had always supported Rick's ventures. "You'll get it figured out and cleaned up."

Cleaning Up the Mess

Rick paid the past-due mortgage payment right away, and he and his new bookkeeper were able to supply financials to the bank the next week. Rick told the bank that he had a plan to make sure the property made money, and the bank gave him ninety days to improve his reporting and operations.

Rick also set up a payment plan for the back taxes, and he told his nephew to either pay the rent or move out. When his nephew moved out, Rick was able to rent to a tax preparer on a long-term lease. All the rents and past NNN charges were collected, and within six months, the property was making money. At that point, Rick repainted the property and seal-coated and restriped the parking lot. It looked and operated like a new property.

All these expenses put Rick behind on his goals of purchasing a new property every three years, but he had learned a valuable lesson in how to manage his investments. Rick now insisted on monthly financial reports from his bookkeeper. He started to think about buying other properties too, and he realized he would want to hire a property manager just to make sure nothing got overlooked. But for the time being, he was content with Zonko's and Molly's now that they were organized and financially successful.

Lessons _____

1. When you manage your own property, remember to have an accounting system (software like QuickBooks or Rent Manager) that tracks your income and expenses by property.

2. Insist that your property manager give you monthly financial reports and go over everyone, so you can spot problems early on

3. Separate your investment finances from your business.

4. All tenants must pay rent and other fees—no matter if they are your own business, family, or a celebrity.

24 HOW TO MANAGE A PROPERTY FROM AFAR

Investor Profile

Names: Daniel and Allison
Property Type: Apartments
Famous Last Words: "The on-site manager will manage the site, so we don't have to."

Daniel and Allison lived in Boca Raton, Florida, where they coached and managed a college baseball team. Their lives were busy, and they loved the fast-paced nature of their work. They'd inherited a sixty-unit apartment property, the Flamingo, in Kansas City, Missouri, a few years before and had thought it would be easy to keep their baseball lives while the apartment complex brought money in too, so they hired an on-site property manager. Unfortunately, the property was not financially successful, so the couple was having trouble making the mortgage payments. They called local Kansas City apartment brokers and property managers and discovered that the market occupancy rate was 90 percent, but their property's occupancy rate was just 60 percent.

"What should we do?" they asked each other.

Long-Distance Ownership

Just like a long-distance romance, faraway business management takes a bit more work. The adage "out of sight, out of mind" rings especially true with real estate investments. Without regular check-ins, Daniel and Allison's property didn't stay at the level they wanted it to—or even at the minimum level they needed it to. But their lives and careers were in Florida, so they weren't going to move to Missouri, and traveling there once a month wasn't feasible, especially during baseball season.

Based on research they did online and in talking to real estate pros in Kansas City, Allison and Daniel realized they had only two realistic choices to more effectively manage the property:

1. Supervise the on-site manager from afar
2. Hire an off-site property manager to supervise the on-site manager

In either case, they couldn't just expect everything to be taken care of without local oversight. They chose the latter option.

Structure for Success

The first thing Daniel and Allison needed to do to reestablish their expectations for the property was to fly to Missouri and make sure it was in rentable condition. Once they inspected it, they discovered that ten of the units weren't rentable—no wonder they had a low occupancy rate. They realized immediately that they needed to invest more money to get those ten units rehabilitated.

They needed to pay attention to the overall appearance of the complex too.

They understood that a property that looked run down wouldn't attract a quality property manager. Even if they paid very well, quality managers wouldn't want to work at a property with moldy walls, leaky ceilings, and overgrown weeds.

Moreover, prospective tenants had multiple apartment complexes to choose from, and a property that looked ragged would not attract new tenants. Not only is a dilapidated property unattractive, but it was also perceived as being less safe than a better-looking complex, so potential tenants would be deterred. So, Allison and Daniel set to work to rehabilitate the Flamingo.

Once they improved the property to rentable condition, they began their search for a reliable off-site property manager. There were quite a few companies to choose from in Kansas City. They knew that they wanted to choose an AMO (Accredited Management Organization) company. These companies have typically been in business for several years and have a well-developed property management infrastructure in place. Daniel and Allison came up with a short list and interviewed several companies. It was critical that they meet with the principals as well as the off-site property manager who would be taking care of their property. At these interviews, they asked how busy the property managers were and if they could handle one more property.

Daniel and Allison were most impressed by Thayer Property Management's level of expertise. They met Elaine, their new potential property manager, and asked her to prepare an annual management plan and draft budget so they could get a sense of how Thayer Property Management would manage the property. In order to prepare this plan, Elaine toured the entire property, inside and out.

Daniel and Allison were pleased with Elaine's management plan and hired Thayer Property Management. As part of the assignment, Elaine helped Daniel and Allison hire a new on-site manager. They needed someone who had a track record of successful on-site property management. To get the right one, Daniel and Allison paid as much as they could and offered health insurance and vacation benefits. Yes, this compensation was expensive, but they'd learned that tenant turnover and unreliable maintenance were more expensive.

Close Monitoring

A few months after Thayer Property Management took over their property, Daniel and Allison requested a meeting with Elaine. They wanted to compare the management plan against the operating results. Elaine provided monthly financial and operational reporting, and the couple was thrilled to see the property was now full—exceeding local tenancy rates. Elaine then worked with them to update the operating goals for the balance of the year.

Daniel and Allison had learned the lesson about long-distance ownership and were committed to fly into Kansas City at least two times a year. In those visits, they met with Elaine and compared notes. Additionally, they had monthly phone calls with her to review financial reports.

With the help of their off-site property manager, a capable on-site manager, and their own closer involvement, Daniel and Allison were able to increase the occupancy of their apartment building to average at least the market occupancy rate of 90 percent, a successful conclusion to a difficult situation.

"It's just like keeping your eye on the ball," Daniel told Allison.

She laughed. "Yeah. I guess we should've seen that one coming, huh?"

By applying this basic baseball principle to their investment, they became much more successful.

Lessons _____

1. If you don't keep an eye on your property, you will have no idea what kind of shape it's in, the kinds of tenants who are renting there, or why you might not be hitting your financial goals.

2. Your property manager needs to be managed too. If your property is far away, either visit often or hire someone local to oversee management.

3. You can write off two trips per year to inspect your property (check with your CPA).

PART IV:

PROTECTING YOURSELF FROM EXTENDED LIABILITY

25 INSURANCE CUSTOMIZATION

Investor Profile

Name: George

Property Type: Property Insurance

Famous Last Words: "I often hear people say, 'Odds are, we won't need insurance for that.' Then they regret it."

George was an experienced insurance broker with a particular expertise in real estate investments. He believed that insurance was a critical piece of risk management for owners of real estate, and the things he'd seen proved that one could never be too careful.

Once a year George would give a seminar to his real estate clients and interested investors to help them understand what their insurance covered and to determine if they needed to be looking at any additional policies.

Anything Can Happen

George began this year's session by relating tales of recent significant issues his clients had faced that he'd been able to help them with.

One of his commercial clients, he told the crowd gathered on a Saturday morning, had a neighborhood shopping center that had a property management company located on-site. A frustrated tenant who was being evicted for not paying rent decided to firebomb the company with a Molotov cocktail. His client was fortunate that the fire department responded quickly, and the building did not catch fire, but there was significant smoke damage.

Several of the attendees nodded knowingly while several others looked horrified.

George went on. In another case a condominium owner decided not only to blow up her car (stored in her garage, under her condo) but also to try to set her unit on fire. George had fortunately talked the client into purchasing extended umbrella insurance.

In one case a tenant moved out of an apartment property but claimed that the appropriate abandonment time was not given for him to remove his goods and that the landlord had wrongly hauled away irreplaceable personal items.

George had experienced nature stepping in to create havoc too. It was not unusual to have pipes break in a sudden winter freeze. In one case the fire sprinklers froze in a commercial building, and the resulting ice expanded and broke the pipes, creating significant water damage as the temperature warmed up.

Insurance Was in Place

Before the shocked seminar attendees decided to run out and sell their properties so these fiascos wouldn't happen to them, George assured them that all situations had ended up okay because the clients had insurance to help cover the damages. In the first case, the tenant's insurance took care of all the smoke damage caused by the tenant's Molotov cocktail. In the second story, both the association and the condominium owner had insurance, so they sorted out who needed to cover the common areas that were affected by the car fire. In the third case, the property management company had errors and omissions insurance in place to cover alleged miscommunications or mismanagement, but they chose to settle the claim out of pocket. In the last situation, the property's insurance covered the water damages, allocating enough money to rehabilitate the suites and cover the emergency response costs.

Out of Pocket

When George paused, one young, clean-cut investor raised his hand. "Why would a property management company settle out of pocket if it had insurance?"

George got this question at almost every seminar, and he was glad this young man had brought it up as an easy transition. He smiled and explained that most property owners take the cost of insurance into consideration when they're choosing their level of coverage. Basically, they try to find a balance between having a deductible that's low enough that they can pay if they really have to, but high enough to keep the monthly payments low. George typically encouraged a larger deductible and having reserves to self-insure for small claims.

"The key here," he said, "is how much cash you have and how much you're willing to tie up as self-insurance."

When he explained that there was no right percentage or fixed number— it just depended on the investor's comfort level and their personal cash balance—the man with the question looked unsatisfied.

George decided to illustrate it with an example. "Let's say a claim was $15,000 and the deductible was $10,000. If you run it through insurance, you still must pay $10,000, and the claim goes on your property loss history. You could directly pay this claim to keep it off your loss history." He talked about LexisNexis's product C.L.U.E. that gave the public—and insurance companies—access to loss histories for properties.

"Plus," he added, "if you have many claims, it might form a pattern that would make insurance carriers less likely to underwrite your properties in the future, and even if you are able to carry insurance, your premiums could be significantly higher, so it pays to be selective about filing insurance claims."

George took a sip of water before adding, "If a claim was $250,000, though, then it makes the most sense to turn the claim over for insurance help."

The man nodded. "So basically, the wealthier you are, the more sense it makes to self-insure for small claims?"

"Exactly."

Buying Insurance

"But how do we know which insurance company to go with?" asked a redheaded woman in the middle row.

"I can help you with that," George assured. He told her he shopped for the best insurance coverage for his clients. Of course, he looked at price, but he also considered an insurance company's financial strength and industry ratings as well as its payment history—how often it paid claims and how long it took to do it.

"In fact," George said, "that's something you can do too. Just go to the state's insurance commissioner website to review the claims payment history of different insurance carriers." He liked to tell his clients this, so they felt empowered to watch out for themselves too. The woman seemed to appreciate that advice and made a note.

"And if for some reason we're not getting results from your insurance carrier, I'll file a grievance for you with the insurance commissioner. Then you're more likely to see the money you're owed, and other people will be warned about troubles with this company."

Residential Investors

"What about houses that are rented out?" one attendee wanted to know. "You've talked mostly about condos and office buildings so far."

"Good question." George smiled and let the room know that renters' insurance and guaranteed replacement cost coverage were must-haves. When a couple people had puzzled looks on their faces, he explained, "A landlord's renters' insurance is different than what tenants carry. For landlords, it's crucial to have this insurance so that if the unit isn't rented for a period and no income is coming in, the insurance helps defer mortgage payments during that time. Guaranteed replacement cost coverage comes into play when a home is severely damaged or destroyed. It covers the cost to rebuild your home given all code and cost changes."

If the policy does not include renters' insurance, then the landlord might be faced with making payments without any income coming in. This is most important for those investors who own rental homes. Typical homeowner policies do not include renters' coverage. George told the group that there were various levels of guaranteed replacement cost coverage, and lower-cost insurance typically paid only for the assessed value of the property as opposed to market value, or replacement cost, of the property.

In closing, George assured his attendees, "I always make sure my clients have enough insurance in place to cover the actual cost of reconstruction and any code and zoning changes, including lost rents coverage for over twelve months."

Several people took George's card and said they'd be scheduling appointments. "I've been handling the deductible-premium ratio all wrong," the young man said. George overheard another person say if she'd had renter's insurance, the past year would have been a lot less stressful. As George packed up, he felt satisfied that he was helping investors protect themselves financially.

Lessons _____

1. Be prepared for tenant damage as well as nature- caused damage by having the right kind of coverage for your properties.

2. Not every issue needs to go through an insurance company. Set some money aside to self-insure for small claims but have good policies in place to take care of large claims.

3. Before you buy insurance, make sure the costs of the deductible and premiums will work for you, but even more importantly, check that the insurance company is reputable.

26 WAKE UP TO LITIGATION PREVENTION

Investor Profile

Names: Kelsey, Wanda, and Rachel
Property Type: Residential Property Management
Famous Last Words: "You can't really prevent being sued."

K elsey, Wanda, and Rachel had seen each other monthly for the past four years. Though their different ages, ethnicities, and lifestyles—evident in their dress and demeanor—made them a curious threesome sitting on the outdoor picnic tables at Brown Dog Barbecue, the ladies had one thing in common: they all worked as on-site managers for Randolf Management Company. As such, they all attended monthly training classes conducted by the residential property management division's vice president, Scott.

After these monthly meetings, the three would meet for lunch to discuss the class and how it pertained to their communities, sharing their experiences to improve their residential workplaces. The training classes focused on a variety of topics, including renting units, dealing with tenant turns, handling maintenance and emergencies, and most importantly, effectively communicating with and responding to tenants.

"When Scott said he got phone calls every month about a tenant who tripped and fell, that was mine," Wanda confessed as she sipped her iced tea.

"Are you kidding me? I thought it was mine!" said Kelsey. "I had one this month too."

Wanda nodded. "Luckily she wasn't hurt too badly and just needed a Band-Aid, some ice, and a couple movie passes to feel better."

"I wasn't so lucky." Kelsey waited for a passing crowd to go by before continuing. "Mine tenant was elderly, and an investigation into the accident needed to be started. I feel so bad."

"Girls," Rachel piped up. "There's only so much we can do, and we do it to the best of our ability." She fiddled with her earrings. "That's why we attend these training sessions: to help mitigate insurance claims and more importantly to prevent them altogether. Our job is all about customer care and maintenance."

Customer Care and Maintenance

"That's how I feel," said Wanda. "Though we live with them like neighbors and can have our own opinion about them in that regard, tenants are customers and need to be respected. I mean, legally we have to."

All three of the women recalled Scott's part of the lecture about the advent of federally funded legal aid, organizations like the Community Alliance of Tenants, and online reviews that tend to stay posted for three to four years.

"It's more important than ever to provide the best possible customer care to tenants," Wanda concluded.

"Do they still have that bad review on you up?" asked Rachel.

"The one that called me a pretentious, money-grubbing snob? Yes, thank you for bringing it up." Wanda laughed awkwardly. "It did teach me a lesson about separating the personal from the professional, though. Even as rude and obnoxious as those tenants' kids were, I would've treated the situation so much better if I'd thought of them as customers and not as the annoying people who lived next door."

"We all make mistakes," said Kelsey. "But as Scott said, by keeping good lines of communication and mutual respect with tenants, we protect ourselves and Randolf from unnecessary litigation over those mistakes or misunderstandings. I just hope it pertains to me in this case." She looked worriedly at her empty iced tea glass, but they all knew her mind was elsewhere.

"It's a no-brainer for him. He sees the numbers, he knows that treating tenants well also pays off in customer loyalty and longer residency, less damage, and fewer new tenant referrals," Wanda pointed out. "But he's so removed that it's easy to preach. We're on the front lines."

"I don't know," said Kelsey. "I think those customer service role-playing exercises he had us do were pretty good, even if I was super awkward saying the lines at first. I'm going to use some of those from now on."

"I like how he said that more than anything, most customers want to feel heard." Wanda smiled as the server approached with their food. "I need to remind myself that the first step is to listen to them and say I'm sorry to hear that they're upset before being reactionary." With a beautiful pulled pork sandwich in front of her, she widened her eyes comically. "I could react to this, though!" They all laughed.

Kelsey dressed her salad while she thought more about the training. "One thing I didn't need more practice doing was preparing an incident report. I'm well aware of how to recognize whether a tenant's fall was severe enough to pass it through insurance. I feel so bad."

She stabbed at some lettuce while Rachel raised her eyebrows. "Really, though, I thought the when-to-report section of the training was self- explanatory. Who can't tell if a tenant's complaint is serious enough to require investigation? And if a maintenance concern is important enough to call for emergency action? Those are things that should be obvious if you have any concern for your tenants."

"Not necessarily." Rachel waved a manicured finger in the air. "When I first started, I couldn't recognize a serious situation versus a merely upset tenant, or how to handle either scenario. I called in everything."

"I guess you can get complacent if you're used to lower standards than Randolf's. Looking around this patio, I see three of the maintenance issues Scott mentioned that might seem minor but could contribute to accidents."

Kelsey pointed out the uneven sidewalk, the loose railing on the stairs leading into the barbecue restaurant, and a paper cup on the patio.

"That wouldn't fly with us," said Wanda. Scott personally inspected all the properties for major maintenance concerns at least once a year but constantly reiterated to the on-site managers that it was their job to watch for these minor issues all the time.

Kelsey got up to put the loose cup in the garbage.

"I guess I should move the stack of newspapers that's by the office door," said Wanda.

"Isn't it funny how we all come out of these meetings thinking of ways to fix all the minor issues we suddenly notice at our properties?" commented Rachel. "Can't have anything to do with the fact that the more we do to prevent litigation, the more we ultimately save the company money, which goes toward our paychecks."

Kelsey and Wanda nodded in agreement.

Law Changes

They ordered another round of iced tea to sip before heading back to their properties.

"Today's training was pretty good," Wanda said. "I like the customer service and basic maintenance tips, but the classes about landlord-tenant law and state and federal laws on discrimination, environmental practices, and safety procedures bore the heck out of me." She bowed her head as if falling asleep in her chair. "I know they're important—so many laws change continually—but most of it we know already, or it's been covered in the annual training sessions."

Wanda could still see the bullet list of all the topics covered in this year's annual legal session at Randolf's:

- Accessibility requirements per the Americans with Disabilities Act

- Assistance animals
- The terrorism watch list
- Discrimination against tenants
- Swimming pool operation
- Underground injection control maintenance
- Material safety data sheets (required by OSHA, the Occupational Safety and Health Administration)
- Smoking policy disclosure
- Asbestos
- Fire codes
- Smoke detectors
- Satellite dishes
- Lead-based paint
- Meth lab cleanup procedures
- Carbon monoxide detectors
- Building codes
- Confidentiality and privacy
- Mold and mildew identification and remediation

One of the reasons all three liked working for the Randolf Management Company had to do with the company's good record and significant commitment to stay informed on the constant changes to the numerous local, state, and federal laws. Scott also managed the company's memberships with national and local organizations that had banded together to hire a lobbyist to ensure that management companies' interests were represented when the legislature met on an annual basis.

"I hear you," Rachel raised her glass. "But hey, at least we work for a company on the forefront of the industry."

They clinked their iced tea glasses, each knowing that it takes work to keep on top of an industry with so many details.

Keeping Current

The most important action Scott took every year was personally inspecting all the properties managed by the Randolf Management

Company. He made sure that the on-site managers and maintenance staff kept the properties clean, easy to navigate, and safe.

He was relentless in his search for perfection, and not all the managers liked his tough attitude, but these three women agreed that they would've liked being sued even less, so they appreciated the fresh set of eyes.

"I just feel so bad about that woman's fall because I know it could've been prevented," said Kelsey. The meal was winding down and they all needed to get back to work, but she still felt the need to talk out what was going on with the investigation. "And even worse, Scott knows it could've been prevented. I had several apartments move out at once and needed all the units painted, so I was busy coordinating minor maintenance when Scott came through. He mentioned that one of the two steps on the outside walk leading up to the units had this loose tread. I told him I had it covered because it had happened before. I just needed to get to it, but really, I wasn't in too big of a rush because it was in the corner of the stair where nobody would put their foot. A couple days later, this lady tried to balance her cane on it and fell."

"Ouch." Rachel cringed. "I once had an issue with a house owner who didn't have the money to make necessary repairs," she said. "Scott found a line of credit—or maybe it was a hard money loan, I can't remember.

"Anyway, that enabled that client to improve his property and reduce the potential for risk. Sometimes if you're overwhelmed or can't do something for yourself that you know is in the best interest of the property, ask Scott. That's what he's there for."

Kelsey nodded, obviously still upset.

"Kelsey, you're a sweetheart," Wanda tried to reassure her. "You respect, respond to, and communicate with your tenants, and they all love you. Did you have any issues with this older lady who fell?"

"No," said Kelsey. "She was the one hurt and she kept telling me that it would be all right. I guess I was pretty upset."

"That settles it. You probably don't have anything to worry about. Tenants who are cared for and appreciated by their property managers wouldn't typically sue over minor issues. They'd work with a manager or landlord to resolve problems," said Wanda.

"More importantly," added Rachel, who had worked as an on-site manager longer than either of the other two, "they proactively bring problems to the attention of the property manager, knowing they'll be treated well."

"Is that why I'm so busy?" Kelsey smiled for the first time.

"But you know what Scott says…" prompted Wanda.

"Be aware of potential liabilities all the time," said the three in unison. This got people's attention at the adjoining tables of Brown Dog Barbecue.

Lessons _____

1. When staff are trained well, they can help prevent and mitigate insurance concerns. Frequent inspections will meet the "necessary standard of care."

2. When tenants feel valued, they're more likely to communicate concerns before major problems happen and less likely to sue.

3. A good property management company can help owners find alternative sources of money to keep the property in good condition.

27 THE TRIBULATIONS OF TRIP, SLIP, AND FALL CLAIMS

Investor Profile

Name: Laura
Property Type: Office Building/House/Apartments
Famous Last Words: "Vendors know how to watch for risks and prevent falls—why would I need to check after them?"

As an owner of a property management company, Laura was faced with daily challenges. She kept a logbook to keep all the various issues well documented, so she could learn from each one, hopefully preventing similar situations from arising again.

The main issue that seemed to keep coming back to haunt her was litigation surrounding tenants or visitors tripping, though. She went back into her logbook to reread the details on the three biggest issues she'd faced. Here are some notations out of her logbook.

Roadwalk Plaza

I decided to have the interior walls of the Roadwalk Plaza, a 30,000-square-foot office building, painted. It had been years since the walls and ceilings had been touched up, and the building was looking shabby. I hired a painter and completed what I thought was all the preparatory work. He showed up, set up, and pulled out a plastic sheet to cover the carpeting in case some paint spilled.

It was the end of the day, and the telephone rang in our office. Mr. and Mrs. Smith called in an accident. They had just left their office on the second floor when Mrs. Smith slipped on the plastic and fell down the stairs. She hadn't been holding on to the handrail because she didn't want to get close to the walls where she might get paint on her new coat.

Mr. Smith first called 911 for his wife, and then he thought to call me. I immediately called the painter, who realized that his crew had not pulled up the plastic before they had gone home for the night. He rushed over to remove the plastic to prevent any further injuries.

Thirty days later, the Smiths sued the owner of the building, the painter, and my property management company. According to the paperwork, Mrs. Smith's damages included a broken tailbone, pain and suffering, and loss of consortium. Of course, we tendered our defense to our insurance company, but it would have been better to prevent the entire situation by making sure the painter had removed the plastic covering over the carpeting. Our insurance company took care of the claim.

Rockfield Street

Margaret, the tenant in the house on Rockfield Street, called and told me her daughter had slipped and fallen on the deck of her rental house. She wanted me to pay the medical bills.

I had just installed a new deck and steps for the house, which I wanted to have finished before the rainy season began, but I didn't quite make it. The deck had been painted with a coat of primer, but we hadn't yet put on the gritty finish coat to prevent slipping—it was raining too much to do it.

I reported the slip-and-fall incident to my client's insurance agent, who resolved the claim and made sure all the medical bills were paid for in an attempt to preclude a lawsuit from Margaret's attorney.

Silverton Garden Apartments

Irene, our contracted cleaning person, was preparing an apartment for re-rental. She brought her husband, who was eighty years old, along to help, and he tripped and fell off the sidewalk, breaking his hip. Irene should've had her own workers' compensation insurance, but she didn't. So, she sued me for $500,000, and because I was covered by the client's insurance as part of the management agreement, I tendered the claim to the client's insurance company.

His insurance company refused to cover the claim, so I had to involve more attorneys, (thankfully we were covered through our E and O (errors and omissions) insurance) to get it resolved. After six months, Irene's husband was fully healed, the $500,000 claim was settled for less than $20,000, and the E and O coverage was able to be made whole by the client's insurance carrier.

Prevention and Risk Management

Laura noted that in each of these cases, an accident was involved. She wondered if they could've been prevented. After all, she couldn't hold every tenant's or vendor's hand to make sure they didn't trip. Still, she probably could've checked to make sure the painter picked up his drop cloth, had her deck-building crew warn the tenants regarding the slipperiness of the deck, and double-checked that Irene had her own workers' compensation insurance. She made a mental note to cover preventative measures with all vendors and to emphasize that they were responsible for minimizing accident risks. Beyond that, though, she knew she needed to be personally involved in such projects to watch for potential issues that the vendors may have missed. Laura was glad she and her clients always had insurance and good legal representation, though, and she vowed to never let that lapse.

Lessons _____

1. Because accidents can happen to anyone and on any kind of property, it's critical to have solid, high-rated insurance both as a property manager and as an investor.

2. Hire vendors who understand liability risks, and plan spot inspections to identify slip-and-fall risks.

3. Make sure your vendors carry their own insurance to cover their work and their potential liability.

28 BUSINESS OWNER'S INSURANCE POLICIES FOR NEWBIES

Investor Profile

Names: Roshan and Anita
Property Type: Commercial Building
Famous Last Words: "It's quick and easy to get insurance for a new property."

Sisters Roshan and Anita were buying a commercial property—their first real estate investment without the help of their parents. As they sat at the escrow table ready to sign off, the escrow agent asked them if they carried insurance. They looked at each other and paused, realizing they'd each thought the other had taken care of that.

Quickly Anita grabbed her cell phone and hit the speed dial number for her insurance agent.

"Glenn, I need insurance on the property Roshan and I just purchased. Can you help me?" She was sure he could—he'd been their family's insurance agent for years.

Glenn sensed her urgency and responded quickly with "Do you need a business owner's policy—a BOP—or a homeowner's policy?"

Anita looked at the escrow agent and asked, "Does the bank require that we have a BOP?" When the agent nodded, Anita returned to Glenn.

"Yes, we need a BOP…but can you please remind me what a BOP is?"

BOP Coverage

"Of course but let me pull some information together first." Glenn asked Anita some critical questions about the kind of property that was being insured and the building replacement values. He then confirmed her deductible and the ownership entity, and finally he outlined what coverage was usually included in a standard business owner's policy:

- Accounts receivable
- Sewer and drain backup
- Building ordinance and law coverage
- Lost business income (including loss of rents)
- Debris removal
- Tree debris removal
- Employee dishonesty
- Forgery and alterations
- Money order and counterfeit currency
- Extended replacement costs
- Mold, fungi, wet rot, dry rot, bacteria
- Outdoor property
- Water damage
- Loss of documents (in a flood or fire, for example)
- Liability
- Medical payments
- Pollutant cleanup
- Non-owned auto liability
- Personal and advertising injury liability
- Spouse as insured
- Earthquake
- Flood
- Storm/tornado
- Terrorist

Fine Print

Glenn then continued, "I think this covers your situation pretty well, but can you think of anything this policy excludes that you want to buy extra endorsements to cover?"

Anita couldn't, and she could see that the escrow agent was waiting patiently, so she told Glenn to go ahead with it. She felt a little rushed, but her family had worked with Glenn for years, and he'd always made sure they were well taken care of.

"There's a force majeure clause too, which basically says that the insurance coverage is not effective in case of war or unforeseeable acts of nature. Will this work for you?"

Anita said, "Yes, yes. Let's finalize it."

Glenn patiently reminded her, "As you purchase insurance, remember you are protecting yourself against specific losses."

When the escrow agent started stacking her papers as though she wanted to pack them up, Anita tried to rush Glenn. "We're at the closing table right now, and they won't let us close without proper insurance!"

Glenn replied, "I understand, but I need to look at the property to make sure I can insure it, and I have to look at the loss history before my company will let me even quote the insurance. Give me a minute." Anita was squirming at the table, and she whispered to Roshan, "I think it might take a while to get insurance."

Glenn then spoke again, "Okay, I see the property on the internet. Is it fully rented?" He also needed Anita and Roshan to send him information regarding the tenants. He wanted to know if they all used the same lease, if there was a property manager, which bank was providing the financing, and what its specific insurance requirements were.

Anita spoke quickly into the phone and gave Glenn the details. He pondered. "Look, Anita, I know you're in a rush, but this really isn't something that can go any faster. Let me bind this for a week so no one else can do anything with this property while we get all of the relevant information and you can close."

The escrow agent nodded. "I thought this might happen. It's no problem—just have him email me the temporary binder, and we'll meet again in a week."

Anita could see that Roshan was disappointed that the sale wouldn't happen right away, but she knew Glenn was right—they needed to make sure they got the insurance taken care of properly or else they might regret it later.

Property Management

Later in the day, Anita got an email from Glenn pointing out one more detail they needed to consider about insurance—property management. He wrote:

"If your property is managed by a property management company, understand what the management company's insurance covers. Also, analyze what is discussed in the property management agreement. Typically, the owner of the property co-insures the property manager for liability issues like trip-and-fall incidents.

"If there's on-site staff that works for the property manager, the manager will be responsible for, and may carry insurance coverage for, the following:

- Employee dishonesty
- Employee fraud
- Tenant discrimination (if the landlord is not the one who rented to the tenants)
- Illegal employment practices

"Lastly, confirm the insurance coverage. Property management companies have a range of insurance they carry. Often, though, property managers will limit their exposure, which means you need to cover the gap."

Anita read the email aloud to Roshan, whose face showed how much her mind was spinning. "There's so much to learn. I don't remember all this happening when we bought with our parents. I guess they took care of it all for us."

Anita agreed. "But thank goodness we have Glenn to walk us through it!" Then she emailed Glenn to confirm an appointment for the next day, so they could fully understand all the ins and outs of a business owner's policy.

Lessons _____

1. You need insurance before you meet to sign final closing paperwork.

2. There are different kinds of insurance plans and lots of variables in each one. You can't possibly understand it all in a few minutes. Allow yourself some time for that.

3. A good insurance agent will make sure you understand everything about your policy and what it does or does not cover before you sign off on it.

29 MANAGING YOUR REAL ESTATE RISKS

Investor Profile

Name: Raef

Property Type: Residential/Commercial

Famous Last Words: "Grandpa thinks I'll be an amazing real estate manager like him, but I feel pretty clueless."

Jacob decided the time had come to retire and pass on his small real estate empire to his grandson Raef. Raef had always idolized his grandfather, and Jacob had always had an affinity for Raef, but the boy had a few flaws, namely a somewhat rash temperament and an overabundance of confidence. Though Jacob appreciated his grandson's ambition and had every intention of handing his business over to him one day, he first wanted to make sure that Raef learned the business inside and out. So he brought his grandson on as an apprentice. Every day, Raef reported to his grandfather's home office and followed Jacob's carefully plotted directions.

One day, Raef arrived on time as usual, and Jacob asked him to fetch a binder titled Brickyard Square as he walked through the door.

"What's going on at the Yard?" Raef asked about the 30,000-square-foot commercial property.

"We're going to be sued," Jacob said.

The color drained from Raef's face. Jacob tried not to smile. "That is, unless you find the insurance policy."

"But...you've owned that property forever. It's paid off...the banks no longer require insurance." Raef's voice gradually escalated in panic.

"Sad, isn't it?" said Jacob. "It can take years to build up a successful property and only moments to lose it if an accident were to happen." He paused to let the effect of his words settle in on his grandson. "Luckily there's something we can do about it. In my opinion, risk management is the most important factor in successfully owning real estate, and insurance coverage is our first line of defense in protecting our asset base."

Insurance

Jacob had started investing in real estate in a small way. He'd learned the business hands-on and knew Raef would need hands-on experience too—that was the only way he'd grasp the important points.

Jacob said to Raef, "Back when I was an investor with a small portfolio—a rental house, a duplex, and a small retail building—I bought landlord insurance policies to deal with fires, building damage, and the like. I filed them away in those binders, adding new copies when they were renewed. Now find me the most current policy and tell me what it covers."

Raef shuffled through the papers. Jacob watched him pass the section multiple times until he slowed down enough to find it. Finally, Raef listed, "fire, lightning, explosion, earthquake, storm, flood, escape of water/oil, subsidence, theft, and malicious damage."

"Are you sure that's it?" Jacob asked.

Raef gave the documents more attention and found a few more items: "accidental damage, malicious damage by tenant, terrorism."

"No legal protection? Darn it, we're done for." Jacob said and feigned concern.

Now Raef took care to read beyond the bold points, tracing the lines with his finger, finally blurting out, "Legal protection, Grandpa. It does cover legal protection!"

"You bet it does," Jacob said calmly. "Now grab the Shady Grove binder. We had an issue with one of the units in that storm the other night. Tell me if our policy covers alternative accommodation costs, contents insurance, rent guarantee insurance, and liability insurance."

Somewhat suspicious that his grandfather was sending him on fool's errands, Raef opened the other binder for the twenty-unit apartment property. "Do you get commercial insurance from one company and residential from another?" he asked, noticing the difference in the paperwork.

"Sometimes it works that way. Every time you need insurance, you always want to review a few companies and compare their coverage— don't just default to the company you've used before. You'll need your insurance agent to carefully define and explain the different kinds of policy coverage to make sure the policy includes at the very least liability insurance, property insurance, and loss of rents coverage."

Raef nodded. "Luckily you already have your insurance policies set up. Thank you, Grandpa."

"Funny you should mention that, because in addition to making sure we have legal protection for Brickyard Square, we also have a renewal due, and I want you to run a comparison study for me."

"But why can't I just continue the insurance we have?" asked Raef.

Jacob smiled. His grandson was thinking critically, which was good, but he had so much to learn. "For a couple reasons. First, laws and risks change all the time. Fifty years ago, I didn't need to worry about potentially having to cover cleanup of a property if a tenant turned it into a meth house. These days, that's pretty important. So, you'll need to update the policies from time to time."

"Oh, that does make sense." Raef tapped his fingers on the binder rings. "Plus, I'll probably want to buy new properties at some point, and I'll want to know how to set up the insurance on those."

"My point exactly," Jacob said and reminded Raef to keep looking through the Shady Grove binder.

"What are all these single pages? They have different dates than the policies. Should I pay attention to them?" Raef asked.

"They're riders," Jacob explained. "Riders help you customize insurance policies, and this particular one helps protect you in case a tenant accuses you for discriminating illegally based on age, sex, race, religion, or sexual orientation. You'll want to include a rider for discrimination on any of the residential properties."

When Raef found the coverage information and read it aloud to his grandfather, Jacob sadly shook his head. "That won't be enough to cover the tree that so rudely intruded in our tenant's apartment during the windstorm. Too bad we didn't have an umbrella policy on that property." He swiveled his chair away from Raef muttering, "Shady Grove, should have known those trees would do us in one day..." and pretended to look wistfully out the window while watching his grandson out of the corner of his eye.

Raef was hastily flipping through the binder pages, and Jacob could see his lips silently mouthing, "Umbrella policy, umbrella policy, now where did I see..." He snapped his head up. "Got it! You have $1 million in umbrella insurance coverage!"

"But when does it kick in?" Jacob slowly turned to his grandson.

Fast on the hunt now, Raef scoured the fine print for the information.

"Grandpa, our troubles are over at both properties. We have an umbrella policy—doesn't that cover all your properties?" he asked when he found it.

"No, that won't help our Brickyard Square woes. The umbrella is tied to the property, not the personal property insurance," Jacob explained.

He reminded Raef why the policy was valuable for Shady Grove, though.

"Landlord insurance policies typically don't cover any personal property belonging to tenants, nor do they otherwise protect the interest of tenants, although a liability policy protecting a landlord or property manager will be of benefit to tenants if, say, a visitor comes over, trips, and injures themselves."

"Ah, that makes sense. What about nonresidential properties, though?" Raef asked, still worried about Brickyard.

Jacob was happy to hear Raef starting to grasp the big picture, but he resisted the temptation to lecture. Instead he nudged the Brickyard Square binder toward his grandson and asked him to count all the different policies in the binder. Raef found four, and then with his grandfather's encouragement to look deeper, he found two more, and then two more:

- General liability insurance
- Property insurance (in this case, including a landlord policy for loss of rents)
- Business owner's policy (BOP)
- Umbrella insurance (personal and property specific)
- Tenant discrimination insurance
- Earthquake coverage
- Flood insurance (due to frequent flooding in the area)
- Workers' compensation insurance (because he employed on-site staff and was not using a property management company)

"But that's not all," Jacob said. Raef's shoulders dropped in disappointment as he went back to thumb through the binder for a fourth time when Jacob interjected, "You clearly will want to encourage residential tenants to carry renters' insurance, and that's one thing you won't find in any of our property binders."

Separation between Personal and Professional

Thumbing through all the paper filling just these two binders, Raef teased, "Okay, Grandpa, I know how much you love paper, but in today's world, business has been simplified. People bundle packages of services and store them in the cloud electronically. I can look up my bank account on my phone and find all my accounts, including my investment accounts. I'm sure modern insurance is the same and we can streamline some of this."

Jacob no longer felt bad for the lesson he'd just subjected his grandson to. The young man obviously needed more. "Sure, file things electronically—that's the wave of the future, but make sure you have backups for redundancy." Jacob was amused at Raef's annoyed look. "One thing that isn't redundant, though, is personal and property-specific insurance. What's the name of my company?"

"Which company?" Raef asked.

"Exactly."

Raef chuckled, recognizing that his grandfather was playing a bit of a game. "I did go to business school. I know LLC stands for limited liability company and you form LLCs so that if you're sued, and your insurance doesn't cover the claim, the plaintiffs can only go after the assets in the property-specific LLC, not your personal assets." He paused, considering each of his grandfather's businesses. "But I'm wondering why you manage each property as its own LLC, a separate entity with separate tax returns, insurance, checkbooks, bookkeeping, and annual meetings. Besides, in most states LLCs have annual tax and registration costs, which I'm sure add up. Why don't you bunch commercial properties into one LLC and residential into another?"

"Because this problem at Shady Grove would sink my rental houses," Jacob explained. "Including the one you live in. Don't let tax and registration costs keep you from protecting your assets. If you combine the assets into one LLC, then all your properties become liable if one of the properties has a loss—for example, if there is a trip and fall or we get sued."

At the thought of being kicked out of his house, Raef was stunned into silence, and Jacob could see his lesson had hit home. "It's a lot of details, I know," Jacob went on. "This is basic stuff that I deal with every day, but I have good advisors, and I'll introduce you to all of them. We make decisions together."

Raef relaxed into his usual carefree nature. "Yeah, and most litigation at the property level happens because of deferred maintenance or neglect. We keep our properties well maintained and consistently enforce the rules—more than any apartment complex I've ever lived in! And that attracts better tenants, and quality tenants mean less risk…and you select tenants through a thoughtful and fair process without discrimination, and all that reduces your liability. It's like if you follow the rules of the road and keep your car in good condition, you have fewer chances of an accident and lower insurance premiums to pay."

His grandfather winked approvingly.

Property Management

Then Jacob leaned forward as if to tell Raef a secret. "I haven't worked in years." His grandson gave him a quizzical look. "I used to manage the properties myself, but after a while, I started using Ron Smith's property management company. That's why our properties are well maintained, our rules are enforced, and our tenant selection is so standardized. I can't be in a million places at once."

"Oh, I knew that," Raef said.

"But Ron's about my age, and there will come a time when his company will restructure and, depending on how that goes, you may need to find another property manager."

"Well, no offense, Grandpa, but I'm young, have lots of energy, and with all the good lessons you taught me, I just might want to be more hands-on."

Raef smiled and crossed his arms, asserting his independence. "Then what did you buy all that ski gear for?" Jacob asked.

"Our trip to Vail—you know that," Raef said. "We go every year."

"And your girlfriend's family is from—where, again? You get a house on the beach there every summer..." Jacob pretended to forget.

"San Diego," Raef answered.

"And after you travel to Paris for your honeymoon, you said you were going to visit another world city for every anniversary, right?"

Raef tapped his fingers on his elbows. "Well, that's because she couldn't decide which one she wanted to go to for our honeymoon, but I get it—I wouldn't be able to do any of those things if I self-managed," he said.

"I'm not saying you're hamstrung, but I find that property management companies are a huge boon to property owners. When it's time to hire a new one, it's a good idea to shop around, but make sure you hire an accredited management organization. These are accredited through the Institute of Real Estate Management, and you get to benefit from the

AMO (Accredited Management Organization) insurance that the property manager must carry."

Raef could feel it coming, and sure enough, Jacob asked him to fetch the Ron Smith binder, look up the AMO insurance info, and name the two types of crime insurance. Raef read it out loud:

- A fidelity bond (employee dishonesty) covering all management employees, officers, and owners of the firm in an amount equal to at least 10 percent of the firm's gross monthly collections
- Depositor's forgery and alterations insurance
- Jacob also predictably asked him to cite what other insurance the property management company carried. This time Raef found them all on the first try:
- Errors and omissions
- Employee dishonesty
- Employee fraud
- Tenant discrimination
- Illegal employment practices

Jacob tapped his hand on the table absently. "Ron Smith carries all of these. That's why I do business with him. Of course, you'll need to confirm the insurance coverage for each management company you want to do business with, as there's no industry standard. Often, property managers limit their exposure to your risks through language in their management agreement, which is standard business practice."

Jacob added that the AMO designation also means that the property management company has subscribed to the IREM (Institute of Real Estate Management) Ethics Hearing and Discipline Board, which creates a higher level of responsibility. Raef was relieved when his grandfather did not ask him to look those details up.

Attorney

Raef's mind, however, was still stuck on the fear of being sued. "So back to Brickyard and Shady Grove. Is the insurance enough that we won't get sued?"

Jacob replied, "If the insurance company covers the claims, it will appoint an experienced attorney to defend us as necessary. If it's a smaller claim below our deductible or a claim that our insurance doesn't cover—which you confirmed that it did, but for the sake of argument, let's say it didn't—we would hire an experienced attorney who can protect our interests."

Raef nodded.

"Just one last word of advice, though," Jacob said. "After I'm gone, and you want to make all these newfangled changes, don't hire an inexperienced attorney. Hire one with business law and real estate experience. Spend a little more to take advantage of that experience. Our family attorney, Ms. Maria Torgert, would be a good person to visit with if you have any questions about legal issues."

"So, what do you think? Will we need Maria?" Raef asked.

"You mean Ms. Torgert?" Jacob corrected.

"Yeah, for Shady Grove and Brickyard. What happened at Brickyard, by the way?"

"No, we won't need her this time." Jacob smiled. "Nothing happened at Brickyard, but I do need to renew the general liability policy soon, so it's good that we have the binder out. And Shady Grove is okay too. We just discovered a leaky window during the storm. It didn't cause too much water damage, but it did bring up a potential construction defect issue." When he saw Raef's eyes dart to the clock, Jacob assured him, "We'll start that lesson after lunch. Are you in the mood for teriyaki?"

Lessons _____

1. Owning real property is fraught with risk. Always keep risk management in mind.

2. Protect yourself by making sure you have appropriate insurance policies for each property and check in on these annually to ensure you don't need to make any changes.

3. Register each property as its own LLC to make sure that if it's sued for some reason, only the assets of that specific property are at risk.

4. Keep your property in good repair, hire a great property management company, and if ever the need arises, hire a competent attorney.

PART V:

HOW TO PLAN TO EXIT FROM YOUR INVESTMENTS

30 REPOSITION ASSETS AND SIMPLIFY YOUR LIFE

Investor Profile

Name: Skip
Property Type: Multifamily
Famous Last Words: "I've built my empire, but my family won't know how to take care of it."

Skip had spent the past fifty years investing in multifamily properties to build his real estate legacy. As he sat in the oncologist's office yet again, he felt a myriad of emotions—grateful he'd worked hard when he was younger and didn't have to anymore, relieved that his family would be taken care of after he was gone, sad to be stepping back from his real estate life, and an odd mixture of fear and resignation that the cancer had advanced this far.

The doctor returned with his clipboard and told Skip it would be a good idea to be getting his affairs in order over the next few months. Honestly the cancer didn't scare Skip as much as the prospect of the paperwork Althea and Janet would have to go through after his demise. His wife, Althea, was a handicapped stroke victim, and his daughter, Janet, was the single mother of a son with cerebral palsy. As he left the doctor's office, Skip resolved to take care of everything he could for them.

Exit Strategy

As every real estate investor knows, there are many exit strategies. Skip knew he wanted to keep a stream of income for his wife and daughter but also knew they wouldn't have the time or energy to manage real estate the way he had. He wondered if maybe he should just sell the properties and set the money aside for Althea and Janet to live on.

Selling Real Estate Investments

As Skip trimmed his rose bushes at home, he seriously considered the option of selling his properties. It would be a very nice sum of money for his family, but it would stop generating money in the future—except interest, which wasn't exactly adding up to much these days.

As Skip examined a bloom on his prizewinning Bon Silene rosebush, it dawned on him that selling his properties would also generate a very large sum of money for the IRS. He'd had all the properties for more than a year, so for each, he'd have to pay:

- Federal capital gains tax
- Federal Medicare tax
- State capital gains tax
- Real estate transfer tax
- Local city and county business taxes
- Federal depreciation recapture (in relation to the depreciation write-down over the life of the ownership of the property)

No, this didn't seem like the right real estate exit strategy to enable Skip to take care of his family after he was gone.

Repositioning the Portfolio

Skip moved on to the bright-yellow Mrs. Oakley Fisher rosebush. Suddenly he wished he'd created a new rose breed to name after Althea, but he'd been too busy with his career as a developer and managing his real estate interests, which weren't bad things. All he'd had time for in the garden was the basic maintenance of these rosebushes. He thought it was funny how his values changed as he got older.

Repositioning—that was an idea he hadn't thought of for his real estate situation. He could simplify his real estate portfolio by repositioning his assets. He could set up how they'd be managed, and then Althea and Janet would maintain a stream of income without having to do much.

Skip decided to trade into quality triple-net (NNN) investments with long-term leases. Over the course of the next few months, Skip found several single-tenant listings in medical, retail, industrial, and office buildings. He knew they weren't entirely without risk due to potential market changes, but his main criterion was that the management be low stress.

Unfortunately, he found that his NNN long-term leases didn't have the same flexibility as his residential investments. The rents typically increased only 10 percent over a five-year period with adjustments coming at the lease anniversary mark. The NNN leases meant that the tenants picked up almost all the costs of taking care of their buildings.

In the end, Skip invested in NNN properties in great locations with financially strong tenants. He traded the higher yield of his multifamily properties for lower yield NNNs, but benefitted from long-term tenants, an easy monthly check, and no midnight calls for maintenance.

He'd still have to train Janet to deal with the issues that might come up, especially since so far, she had no experience or interest in real estate. But when he asked her if she was open to it, she was agreeable. "Of course—I'll do what I can to carry it on the way you want and make sure Mom's taken care of. I appreciate that you've set this up for us." She had tears in her eyes.

With that, Skip set to work meeting with his daughter once a week to give her the foundation of knowledge she would need, as well as writing it out for her so she'd have something to refer to after he was gone. He also let his lifelong friends Judd and Arthur know his family's situation, so they could act as real estate mentors for Janet if she needed their help. When it was all in place, Skip felt satisfied that his family would live in comfort after he was no longer there to provide for them. With his real estate issues resolved, he went about trying to develop a hybrid rose for Althea.

Lessons _____

1. There are several options for passing on your real estate legacy and taking care of your family. Consider your priorities as well as those of the family members who will be taking care of the properties.

2. Selling can generate a lump sum return, but don't forget about the taxes you will have to pay.

3. Repositioning assets can help minimize the work your family has to do while also keeping a stream of income for them.

31 PASSING REAL ESTATE ASSETS ON TO THE NEXT GENERATION

Investor Profile

Name: Judd
Property Type: Commercial Buildings
Famous Last Words: "It's time to retire. I'll sell my shares to my partners, so I can cash out and spend my days in peace."

W hen Judd's friend Skip brought up his real estate exit strategy, Judd realized he too ought to be thinking about how he would simplify his investments. He didn't have a family to take care of like Skip did, but he was growing older and didn't want to spend so much of his time and effort taking care of real estate details.

Unlike Skip, Judd wasn't the sole owner of his properties. He'd always liked working with partners, and he'd built his legacy by investing in commercial properties with a few other investors he trusted. Maybe the easy option was to simply sell his shares to those partners.

Selling to Partners

Although Judd completely trusted his partners as investors and as friends, he had witnessed plenty of seemingly perfect partnerships ending in disputes, unfair division of assets, and even sticking one partner with the taxes and debt while the other partners kept the profit. Fortunately, he had insisted on having a very good attorney manage all the partnership agreements, so he felt reasonably confident that none of these devastating scenarios would happen to him if he were to sell.

However, Judd started to have the same realization that Skip had had—selling his share in his partnerships would generate cash, he would have to pay a lot of taxes and he'd no longer have a consistent stream of income. He realized he didn't really want to sell, just to simplify. So, he started looking at other types of partnerships and asking his friends and colleagues for their thoughts. That's when he found out about UPREITs.

Investing in an UPREIT

One of Judd's partners, Tom, had him over for dinner to talk about UPREITs. Judd, Tom, and his wife, Sarah, sat down to a delicious spread of Caesar salad, pan-roasted duck, and mashed sweet potatoes. Judd loaded up his fork while Tom first explained that UPREIT stood for umbrella partnership real estate investment trust.

"Basically," Tom said, "you sell your property on the open market using a 1031 exchange, and then you use your 1031 proceeds to invest in a real estate investment trust, or a REIT. Then, by virtue of a 721 exchange, the assets are traded into shares of the REIT."

"That sounds like a roundabout way of doing things," commented Sarah before taking a bite of sweet potatoes.

"It's possible to just trade your investment into a REIT," explained Tom, "but that rarely happens because companies that manage UPREITs want to be able to choose their own property focus."

Judd puzzled over all this while Tom sipped his wine.

"It's actually not that complicated." Tom told him how he'd recently sold a relinquished property and structured a 1031 exchange. Then instead of searching for a suitable replacement property, he identified and acquired a fractional interest (tenant-in-common interest) in real estate that the REIT had already designated. This completed the 1031 exchange portion of the transaction.

All he needed to do then was contribute the fractional interest into the operating partnership after a holding period of twelve to twenty-four months as part of a 721 exchange, which was basically a tax-deferred contribution into a partnership. Tom received an interest in the operating partnership in exchange for his contribution of the real estate and was now effectively part of the REIT.

The duck melted in Judd's mouth, but he brought his mind back to the conversation. "My goal is to simplify my day-to-day life," he admitted. "Are you sure this will do that for me?"

"Well, it has for me," said Tom. "In trade for my property, I received a return on my investment and someone else to manage it for me. I just have to cash the quarterly check, and I don't have to pay capital gains on the sale of the real estate asset."

Judd nodded, thinking that did sound like just what he was looking for.

By now, Tom was on a roll. "There are numerous other benefits to UPREITs as well." He explained that they provided a viable tax-deferral/avoidance exit strategy to anyone facing significant capital gains tax liabilities on the sale of appreciated property with a low tax basis. They also allowed diversification of real estate holdings.

Judd wanted clarification on that. "Meaning unit holders have an interest in a portfolio of properties instead of just one specific property?"

"Exactly." Tom smiled.

Tom also pointed out that UPREITs gave the potential to convert a liquid, long-term asset into a more saleable security (for example, operating partnership, or OP, units → REIT share → cash), eliminate or reduce property management responsibilities and concerns, provide quarterly income distributions, provide potential to recognize unrealized gains as earnings, provide professional management and expertise in capital markets, avoid risk of negative cash flow, establish estate simplification, allow the owner to dispose of property in a way that maximizes its value, and improve cash position through potential leveraging of OP units.

"If that's all true, it sounds like restructuring my real estate assets in UPREITs will make them easier to give away after I'm gone," said Judd.

"If structured correctly, ownership in UPREITs might not result in a taxable event until the shares are sold," said Tom. "However," he cautioned, "just like you would when doing business with any other company, you must carefully vet the strength of the company, its history, and its goals as well as the experience of the officers running the REIT. Remember, they're trying to make a buck too."

Judd nodded, already knowledgeable about the importance of caution but appreciating Tom's consideration to mention it.

"Also remember that you're exchanging real estate into a security and therefore you no longer own real estate," Tom said. That was a really important point, Judd realized. Since he would then own a security, he couldn't 1031 exchange out of it to buy other real estate. Any sale or disposition of his interest in an UPREIT would be a taxable transaction and would include deferred capital gains and any depreciation recapture. Also, the REIT—not Judd—would have control over the sale or disposition of the asset. "Some UPREIT sponsors will guarantee that they won't trigger any taxable gain for a specified number of years, but not all."

Sarah got up to clear the plates, but the conversation went on.

Tenant-in-Common Investments

Judd was visibly let down by Tom's last caveat on the UPREITs. He thought he had found the perfect low-maintenance solution for his properties.

Tom tried to reassure him. "Everything has upsides and downsides, and then there's always the workaround. My family got burned badly by TIC investments. I swore I would never consider them again, but now there are some tempting incentives in that market."

"Wait," Judd said. He knew tenant-in-common (TIC) investments were pooled real estate investments that had been hit in the market downturn of 2008, but he also knew how much the market could change. "What's the outlook of TICs now?"

"Well, the problem around 2008 was that the short-term mortgages that financed many TICs needed to be refinanced, but the financial institutions were loath to refinance because vacancy rates had increased, and income had declined. My family lost significant assets due to that meltdown." He emphasized this with a grave nod. "All was not as advertised."

Tom explained in greater detail that the US Securities and Exchange Commission (SEC) decided that these were securities and needed to be sold by stockbrokers with securities licenses instead of real estate agents. But out of this challenge, two companies in Utah, Rockwell and RealtyNet Advisors, decided they could mitigate investment risk by taking investors' 1031 returns and placing them into NNN investments, for which no loan was needed.

"In other words," Tom broke it down, "100 percent of the purchase price for a single-tenant investment comes from 1031 proceeds that investors placed in the pool." They also focused on very small investments in the $1 million range, possibly to avoid securities regulations.

When Sarah brought in the dessert course, Judd's taste buds tingled despite being very full. "So now we're back in the pool, you see. We have less risk because the worst thing that could happen is that the tenant fails, which just means that we end up with an empty building we must fill. We can't lose the building to a financial institution because there's no loan in place. In addition, TIC sponsors mitigate this risk by investing in buildings with only high-quality national tenants. They keep it simple. They collect the rent, charge a management fee, inspect the property, and then send me a check. Since there's no loan, there's no mortgage to pay off, which helps with the upside on the yield. My average returns are about 7 percent."

"And the downsides are?" Judd prodded.

Tom laughed. "The downside is that you're still in a type of a partnership, and when you want to exit from this structure, you have to live by the TIC agreement. Basically, much like with the UPREIT structure, you cede control of the investment to a third party. If the third party mismanages your property, you could lose all the return from your investment."

"Okay," Judd concluded, "so just like with investing with partners, I've got to do my research to make sure the company will handle everything professionally. Good thing I've still got that amazing attorney!"

Judd left the dinner feeling confident that he would find a good UPREIT or TIC arrangement to help him simplify his investments. He might even find one of each, but he decided he better not get ahead of himself.

Lessons _____

1. Sometimes the options that will help you simplify your investments sound the most complicated, but it's worth it to understand them to see if they will work for you.

2. UPREIT and TIC partnership investments can both be good options for making your retirement less complicated if the circumstances work for you; however, do the research to make sure the companies you'll be investing with will honor your best interests. Any investments where you are a minority partner means you are not in control and could have unexpected consequences. For example, if the partnership is sold and you are not ready, you will have to pay capital gains taxes and basis adjustments. These investments are inherently risky and need to be treated with care.

32 FAMILY DYNAMICS

Investor Profile

Name: Arthur
Property Type: Commercial Buildings
Famous Last Words: "Building the empire was easy— deciding what to do with it is the hard part."

A s Arthur aged, he realized early that things needed to change with regard to his real estate investments. He had a solid portfolio of rental houses and some commercial properties, but he had grown weary of dealing with the details involved with the day-to-day operations, and after his heart surgery, he had started having to come to grips with his mortality as well. Never was he more aware of these questions than one cloudy day in September, when he went to play golf with buddies, Skip and Judd.

Arthur had played golf with Skip and Judd since his kids were little, and now his son, Pete, often tagged along hoping to learn some of life's wisdom from his father's golfing buddies. Pete had made some bad decisions in his younger years, which made Arthur nervous as he considered retirement.

Pete had never been intuitive with numbers, and the tax implications involved with selling assets had snagged him in the past. Arthur wished he could've gotten Pete to understand that a direct sale of a property could cost 40 percent or more of the capital return.

Today, though, it was just the three pals out on the green.

"Making decisions regarding the future of real estate investments is much like selling a business," said Judd, stepping up to the first tee. Judd had been Arthur's best friend since elementary school and, of the three of them, the most successful. He'd recently repositioned his assets into UPREITs and TIC partnerships to allow him room to enjoy his retirement more.

Skip nodded from the golf cart. He was looking paler and paler every time Arthur saw him, and he reported that he had just repositioned his assets into NNN investments, so his wife and daughter would be taken care of after he passed.

Arthur felt grateful that he had some time to decide how to transition his assets before he was in Skip's position, but he still felt the pressure to choose the right exit strategy for his investments soon. After all, you never know when something might happen.

Choosing a Path

Arthur was up to his eyeballs reviewing all the different directions he could choose to reposition his real estate investments and reduce the time and energy needed to manage them. He'd listened to the choices that Judd and Skip had made, but they didn't seem like quite the right situation for his family. Arthur, unlike Judd and Skip, had two children, and both had ideas about what to do with his real estate empire.

Although Pete was interested in inheriting and managing the properties, Arthur was nervous about handing over his lifelong investments with Pete's track record. Arthur's daughter, Ashley, had some very different ideas about what the family should do with the properties.

Contributing to a Charitable Organization

Ashley had been involved with nonprofit organizations her whole life. She'd been an active volunteer since childhood and was now a development director for the city's housing authority. She earnestly argued for her father to donate all his properties to a charity via a charitable remainder trust (CRT).

As Arthur lined up for what should have been an easy putt, he remembered how Ashley had pointed out to him that the size of the tax deduction was based on the current market value of the property, not its cost basis. He missed the shot and decided to tell his pals what was on his mind.

"Ashley researched a structure where the CRT would pay me an annuity." Arthur liked the idea of receiving an income for the balance of his life or for a specified term. "And then it distributes what's left over to the charity. As a tax-exempt entity, the CRT would sell the real estate donated tax-free and reinvest the proceeds in income-producing assets."

After he sank his second putting attempt, Arthur said that although the idea of contributing to charity seemed like a good cause, he felt like something wasn't adding up right. "Ashley did tell me I'd have to pay income taxes on the distributions I receive but that each payment could include a combination of ordinary income, capital gains, and tax-free return of principal. She also recommended that the charity could buy an annuity in my name from the proceeds of the sale of the real estate investment."

Skip mentioned that he'd donated his portion of one of his properties to cerebral palsy research, so Arthur asked him to elaborate.

"Well, it's not all as sunny as it seems," Skip said. "You really have to watch out for some critical tax potholes." He went on to explain that one cannot just estimate the value, or the IRS might disallow the donation. If Arthur was going to do it, he needed to substantiate the value with an appraisal as part of the donation process. For properties over $500,000, he'd have to attach an appraisal to the tax return.

Skip went on with more details. If the charity sold the property within three years of the donation, which most did in the first year, and the property sold for less than the appraised value, the IRS would most likely challenge Arthur's deduction.

"And you cannot prearrange the sale of the property before it's donated to the charity," Skip warned. "If you do, the IRS will disallow the donation, and you'll have to pay capital gains taxes."

Finally, he pointed out that donating properties that are free and clear is a cleaner process than donating one with a mortgage still in place. "My attorney cautioned me that I might end up recognizing taxable income for some of the outstanding mortgage's value."

Judd jumped in with some information too. He'd heard that in addition to the tax concerns, many charities were not set up to accept real estate. "They want cash or stocks instead. If they do take real estate, they have to figure out how to manage it and sell it, which is not always easy. Even those charities that do take real estate prefer donations without a mortgage because of the complicated tax implications."

This was all good for Arthur to know—Ashley had only glossed over the tax pitfalls. She had mentioned that it was not unusual to have a home donated to charity with a life estate attached. She'd called it "a gift of a remainder interest with a life estate." Arthur knew that sort of donation took time to process and had to be planned in advance, so he didn't bother asking Skip and Judd about it. He was already leaning away from donating his properties anyway.

They loaded into the golf cart to ride to the next hole.

Family Succession Planning

Now Arthur was thinking about simply passing his investments on to his children. He had a lot to figure out about taking that path, though, too.

Arthur was an orphan raised by his grandparents who had never saved enough for themselves, let alone for their children and grandchildren, so he didn't have a family history model to go by.

As they bumped along the asphalt path, Arthur knew he first had to find a family member who was mature enough, had an interest, and wanted to learn about the family's existing real estate investments. He'd once thought Pete would be this person, but he had lost confidence in Pete.

"Too bad Pete couldn't make it out today," Judd said from the driver's seat.

"Yeah, he wanted to," Arthur said. In truth, Arthur had asked Pete not to come that day because he wanted to talk to his friends about his possible exit strategies without his son there to influence the conversation.

Arthur had forgotten that just like Pete, he too had made many mistakes building his portfolio. He'd expected his son to make the "right" decisions just because he had grown up watching his father's affairs. Arthur had expected his son to learn by example, but he'd never given him any direction about how to make the right decisions. He now knew this to be an unrealistic expectation. Pete needed to be mentored and educated patiently over time. Pete needed a second chance.

Pete had recently taken some real estate finance classes to convince his father that he had matured and was preparing himself for future decision making. Now Arthur concluded he needed to involve Pete in the basics of management such as property inspections, financial reviews, attorney meetings, refinancing, and purchasing decisions. Arthur also needed to draft long- and short-term plans on paper to ensure that Pete and he were on the same page regarding the future of the portfolio.

Arthur recognized that he needed to relinquish control. Pete had come a long way since his low point; he had worked as a fulfillment manager at a frozen food company for over fifteen years now and owned a nice condo. Still, Arthur felt hesitant to let go of planning and decision making. He knew that mistakes would be made, and he considered that relinquishing control a little bit at a time might allow him to share his experiences with Pete in a controlled environment.

Of course, Arthur needed to consider Ashley too. Although he didn't plan to donate the properties as she'd suggested, he needed to include her in his plans to pass his investments on. To make both children stakeholders would involve creating a reasonable reporting relationship and deciding how decisions were going to be made. Additionally, they could develop a dispute-resolution process to prevent either one from capitalizing on the relationship at the expense of the other.

By the ninth hole, the clouds had begun to clear, and the friends' banter moved from real estate to their various families. Though each came from different backgrounds, it was funny how their relatives shared common personality traits, which inevitably complicated the men's investment decisions. Among the three of them, at least two had children, nieces, or nephews who fell into at least one of the following categories:

- A spendthrift
- A very conservative investor
- A very risk-oriented investor
- A very sophisticated investor
- Someone who did not get along with the others
- Someone who needed cash to pay for college
- Someone who needed cash to retire or make a house payment
- Someone with a disability or a mental illness
- Someone who had no interest in real estate at all and was willing to opt out of all decision making
- Someone who had different ideas from the rest of the family

Judd and Skip laughed at these similarities until they noticed Arthur looking worried.

"Don't worry so much," Skip said. "You'll figure out the way to pass everything on to Pete and Ashley."

Judd nodded. "Just keep a level head and work with your advisors. Use some of that hard-earned money"—he rubbed his fingers together in the universal sign for money— "to hire the right people to help you navigate all this."

Arthur laughed. He could always count on his friends to cheer him up. Arthur knew he'd need to plan with his estate and real estate attorneys to build a trust structure that would address the needs of the next generation. His real estate trusts would not last into perpetuity. He also doubted that either of his children would hold on to them long enough to pass them on, but he wanted to set them up so that they would have the opportunity to grow the investments.

Lessons _____

1. You have various options to protect yourself when you're ready to retire from active real estate investing, but there's no one right answer. Your personal situation influences your decisions.

2. Donating real estate to charity is an option, but make sure you understand the taxes involved, and double-check that the charity even wants a real estate donation.

3. To pass your estates on to your children, you'll first need to train them how to thrive in the real estate world. You'll also need to set up decision-making procedures to help them manage your real estate investments together, so no one gets taken advantage of.

33 TRAINING THE NEXT GENERATION OF REAL ESTATE INVESTORS

Investor Profile

Name: Jack

Property Type: Residential/Commercial Buildings

Famous Last Words: "We don't want to bother our kids with our investment details—they have their own careers and stresses."

*F*unny...*I don't feel any older, but who is that man in the mirror?* Jack mused to himself. He turned to his wife and said, "Wow, the last fifty years have really flown by."

"They sure have," she answered.

Jack and his wife, Mae, had spent the afternoon reviewing the details of their real estate portfolio. In over fifty years of investing, they had bootstrapped themselves from one rental house (a shack, more or less) to a portfolio of two large apartment complexes and five commercial buildings, netting them over $25,000 a month.

They had a very comfortable lifestyle and traveled extensively. They'd hired a real estate property management company to take care of their investments, so they received monthly reports, which they reviewed together. Many years earlier they'd made sure to build up significant reserve accounts for each property, planning for taxes, major capital expenses, vacancies that might require significant remodeling, and for the commercial buildings, large leasing commissions.

Life was pretty good, but there was one small problem nagging Jack: he was aging and becoming a little forgetful. He knew they needed to get young blood involved in their investments. The next day he called up his property manager, Emily, and his CPA, Xavier, and asked them for advice. They agreed to meet Jack and Mae for lunch to discuss his concerns.

As they mulled over the problem of succession, Jack and Mae divulged that their three grown children had never been involved in their financial or real estate affairs. As parents, they hadn't wanted to bother them with the details, since they worked full time and had their own stresses with raising children. But there was no denying that their three daughters were very competent and well established in their late forties and early fifties, and with some guidance, they could manage the real estate portfolio well. Still, they had no idea if any of the children were interested in real estate— or investing, for that matter. So, they hatched a plan to find out.

Introducing the Kids to the Portfolio

First Mae and Jack invited their adult children for a weekend visit without their spouses or children. While Mae felt that blood relatives should be making decisions over the real estate assets if possible, this weekend with just the core family, was also about focusing on the future. Jack and Mae wanted as little distraction as possible while the family made these serious considerations. The fewer people at the table and the more focused they were, the easier it was going to be to come to a consensus. Jack and Mae made it very clear that this was a planning session regarding money, aging, and their real estate investments.

As they assembled for a home-cooked dinner on the first night, Jack announced that he and Mae were very pleased that the kids had come to visit and that this was meant to be a weekend of fun, and yes, some hard work thrown in.

"Tonight, is for remembrances. Tomorrow, we work." They had a wonderful dinner and laughed like they hadn't in years. By bedtime, the sisters were wondering what could be so serious that their parents had called them all together so suddenly.

"It's not their health, right?" Jack overheard Nancy, the youngest, ask her sisters in the den. "Mom and Dad never seem to age. They haven't said anything to you, have they?" Her sisters, Donna and Anita, said they hadn't and reassured her that they thought their parents seemed fine, just focused on planning for the future.

After the girls cleared the breakfast dishes the next morning, Jack called the family meeting to order. "A funny thing happened the other day," he began and told a story about how he'd left to drive out to check on one of their commercial buildings. Seeing his favorite bakery on the way, he'd stopped to feed his sweet tooth. When he came home with a cupcake for Mae, she asked him about the property, and that was when he realized he'd totally forgotten his original destination!

"The distraction could happen to anyone," he joked as the whole family laughed. He knew his daughters loved the same bakery, but he used the example to transition to the matter at hand—that he and Mae were aging, and he was having short memory lapses.

When Nancy's eyes grew wide, Jack held up his hand. "Nothing to be so worried about." He laughed. "Just time to start planning for the future."

He explained that their real estate holdings were significant, and that Mae and he wanted them to be passed on to the next generation. For that to be successful, their daughters needed to be involved during a transition period.

Just as the daughters were nodding their understanding, the doorbell rang. Jack announced, "That's our limousine." They gasped in delight. "Now is the time for us to inspect our properties."

As they opened the door to the limo, Jack introduced the daughters to Emily, the property manager, who was coming along for the ride to give a detailed overview of all the properties. Each daughter was given a briefing book, which included property histories, tenant information, condition of the property, latest capital improvements, and individual balance sheets and income statements for each property. The girls were excited and piled into the car with their parents.

Six hours and lunch later, they made it home exhausted. Anita exclaimed, "So much to see, so little time!"

Identifying Passion

Like a retreat leader, Jack directed, "Let's break for a nap and dinner and then resume."

After dinner Jack explained the LLC structure of the investments and the trust structure of their estate. Then they took time to go over their financial statements for the last few years. The kids were impressed with the scope of the assets and the return they generated.

Then Jack said, "What's most important is that we need to train you all, so you understand real estate and can create a process of decision making for the properties and the future managers. In the end, one of you will need to work with Joyce and her team on the day-to-day decisions. Things happen every day at our properties, so that person needs to be able to make the commitment of time and focus. Meanwhile, major decisions over $10,000 and those involving strategy or refinancing, purchasing, or selling properties will probably need to involve all of you as a group.

"Now is the time to devise a family strategy to create consensus and cooperation for now and into the future," Jack went on. "We also need to plan for what happens if one of you dies, or is incapacitated, or just wants out of the partnership after your mother and I have passed away. Our hope is that you'll become as passionate and knowledgeable about real estate investing as we are."

The Training Program

"To that end," Jack continued, "we've devised a training program for all of you. There are two purposes for this training program. One is to teach you all we know for you to make the best decisions possible, and secondly, as a group, we need to establish who has the skills and interest to be the next leader once I can no longer manage this portfolio."

There was silence from the girls.

It's understandable—this is a lot at once, Jack reminded himself as he continued to outline his plan. He explained that there were five parts to the training program:

"We are prepared to pay for you to take basic real estate courses, either online or at a college near you. You will need to pass each class with a B or better.

"Joyce and I are going to put together a weekend orientation for you so that you can understand—in detail—the current condition of the properties, as well as how and why we bought them, and put five-year plans in place for each property. In this way," he explained, "we'll also be setting long-term and short-term goals for asset growth and repositioning of the portfolio.

"On another weekend we will be teaching you real estate mathematics, underwriting of real estate deals, how the financial fundamentals work, pro-forma basics, and how to evaluate property financing to better make purchase, sale, and refinance decisions. We will be evaluating the purchase of five potential properties together," Jack told them.

"We will need to spend one day reviewing and role-playing how to make decisions regarding leasing commercial space; how to handle commercial leases, commercial brokers, and their commissions; and how to evaluate tenant improvement expenses and lease rates.

"Finally, after all of this training," Jack said, "all of you will be able to take a key role in decision making for this portfolio. We will need to modify the LLCs to take your involvement into consideration." Then he smiled sweetly at his wife and said to his daughters, "We will also need to plan for the ramifications of our passing and the potential estate taxes that might arise as a result and how to manage that burden."

When nobody said anything for a moment, Jack continued "I know this is overwhelming, but if we plan carefully, we can see each other, have fun together, and all of you will be financially able to plan for your children's college future and your retirement as well."

Donna caught her breath first. "Wow, Dad, you really are prepared! No memory lapses right now, huh?" she teased and then turned more serious. "I for one am on board." She looked at her sisters, and they nodded too. "But with one condition," Donna continued: "our children can come and so can our spouses. You know everyone wants to visit with their grandma and grandpa."

Jack looked at Mae with a gleam in his eyes. Everyone was on board, and they would get to see more of their grandchildren. That was an extra bonus. "Everyone wins!" he said.

Lessons _____

1. When the time is right, introduce your children to your real estate holdings free of the distractions of their kids or spouses.

2. Identify if your children have an interest or passion in real estate investing.

3. Devise a detailed training program so they completely understand your properties, and the procedures it takes to manage them, before they take them over.

34 MOM LEFT US REAL ESTATE—NOW WHAT DO WE DO WITH IT?

Investor Profile

Name: Gary

Property Type: Various

Famous Last Words: "I know Mom left us assets, but I don't know what we will do with them."

G ary knew no one in the family wanted to have this conversation. It seemed so weird, the three of them sitting in their mom's living room without her, but they didn't like the idea of being in a hotel either. Gary thought it wouldn't be as eerie if their dad was there, but he'd died ten years earlier. Now they were on their own.

The property management company had provided Gary reports on the family's many properties earlier that day. He opened the file to begin reviewing the details as his sister reminisced about the pictures and his brother crunched the numbers on the statements of each property.

Gary could only think about how their mother had worked her whole adult life to establish this real estate legacy. These investments had paid for Gary's and his siblings' college, not to mention provided a lot for their kids and set them up with retirement funds. Their mom had put her blood, sweat, and tears into these investments. Beyond that, she'd spent her final years meeting with attorneys and preparing paperwork to ensure Gary, his brother, and his sister would inherit the properties and know how to manage them.

She had wanted her kids to keep the real estate instead of selling it, so she had decided to leave instructions, what her estate attorney called "managing your estate from the grave."

Best Results

Gary flipped deeper into the file and found detailed notes about the family's real estate plans over the past several years. As his mother aged, she had decided that she needed help managing her real estate investments. Gary and his siblings lived far away, so their mom had turned to a property manager to handle the day-to-day operations of the properties.

As part of the transition process, Gary read, his mom had had the choice of gifting portions of her real estate assets to her kids before she passed away, but eventually she'd decided that the tax benefits were not worth the risk of losing control of her assets.

Gary knew that his mom had had some doubts about their ability to take over her properties. She had always respected their life choices, and she had known that they would feel obligated to assist her if asked, but none of them really had the interest, time, and skill set to take care of the assets the way she did it.

It was her risk taking and entrepreneurial energy that had created this family real estate legacy. She hadn't known if any of them had her drive and focus for real estate. Also, though she'd loved and trusted her kids, she had never confided much in their spouses. Gary had often noticed her change the subject when the topic of real estate came up with their spouses in the room. Maybe she had feared that they would capture her assets. He thought she would have done better to worry about making these assets into a family legacy and helping them embrace the drive that built the real estate portfolio.

Family Legacy

Lost in these thoughts, Gary almost overlooked the letter their mom had left for them. Her attorney had advised her to write a letter to her children to give them the context of past investment decisions, to encourage the establishment of financial cash reserves, and to explain why holding on to the real estate portfolio was a good long-term strategy for the family.

For the next hour, Gary's brother and sister sat riveted as they listed to their mother's words spoken through Gary's voice as he read the letter out loud. All three felt a loyalty to their mother that was so strong, none of them would consider diverging from her directions, at least not in the short term.

"She really thought of everything," Gary said.

His sister nodded. "Hey, check out this picture of us kids in front of the green rental house. I guess Mom and Dad took us over there to play while they worked on it."

They all smiled.

"I remember painting those front steps for a little extra money when I was a teenager," Gary said. Keeping the properties in the family felt right, and he was glad his mom had thought so too.

As Gary got ready for bed, he knew that his mother's careful forethought and reasoning had calmed tensions between the three siblings. He hoped he would be able to plan it out as well when it was time for him to pass his assets on to their kids.

Start Early

Though Gary's children were young, he knew right then and there that he would teach them leadership and real estate management skills to help them continue to live their grandmother's legacy. He knew they wouldn't all have an aptitude for leadership or an interest in real estate or financial analysis. That would take time to develop, but his mom had developed fair and transparent procedures that could be adjusted to the personalities in the next and following generations. She'd also left a legacy big enough to help pay for real estate training and to invest in the assistance of good estate attorneys, property managers, and CPAs. Gary also knew that if he continued in his mother's footsteps, the payoff would be large, not just for himself but also for his children and later generations. His mom had truly left a legacy.

Lessons _____

1. When you're passing on assets, develop a written framework to help guide the next generation in consensus decision making.

2. Write a letter to the next generation laying out a plan and giving tips regarding the investments and how to maximize them.

3. Plan ahead to develop an education curriculum for your children and grandchildren to help them learn how to invest and manage real estate successfully.

GLOSSARY

1031 tax-deferred exchange: From IRC Section 1031, an exchange where an investor sells a property and reinvests the proceeds in a new property. The objective is to defer all capital gains taxes.

721 exchange: An exchange transaction where a direct contribution of the investor's real estate goes into the operating partnership in exchange for an interest in the operating partnership.

ALTA (American Land Title Association) survey: A boundary survey prepared to a set of standards that have been prepared and adopted by the ALTA and ACSM (American Congress on Surveying and Mapping). An ALTA survey shows improvements, easements, rights-of-way, and other elements impacting the ownership of land. An ALTA survey is often prepared for commercial properties in order to provide a title company with information required to insure the title to the land and improvements.

Americans with Disabilities Act (ADA): Signed into law on July 26, 1990, the act prohibits discrimination against people with disabilities. Regarding real estate, ADA legislation has been written to make all real property accessible to those who have handicaps.

AMO (Accredited Management Organizations): The only recognition of excellence given to real estate management firms. It is assigned by the Institute of Real Estate Management.

Annuity: A product typically sold by insurance companies that is designed to accept investor contributions, grow funds from an individual, and pay out a stream of payments to the individual in the future, potentially as part of a retirement plan.

Appreciation: As used in real estate, it is an increase in value.

Business Owner's Policy (BOP): An insurance package that assembles the basic coverages required by a business owner in one bundle. Business owner's policies usually target small and medium-sized businesses and typically contain business interruption insurance, which provides reimbursement for up to a year of lost revenue resulting from an insured property rental income loss.

CAM: See Common Area Expenses

Capital expenses: Major building improvements like new roofing or new windows that are replaced rather than repaired. These improvements are considered depreciable and are not expensed. A CPA can clarify. Capital expenses are below-the-line costs when it comes to taking care of real estate and are not included in regular operational income statements.

Cash return: The return of a down payment plus closing expenses delivered to an investor when operating a real estate investment.

CCIM (Certified Commercial Investment Member): A recognized expert in the commercial and investment real estate industry. The CCIM lapel pin is earned after successfully completing a designation process that ensures CCIMs are proficient not only in theory but also in practice. This elite corps includes brokers, leasing professionals, investment counselors, asset managers, appraisers, corporate real estate executives, property managers, developers, institutional investors, commercial lenders, attorneys, bankers, and other allied professionals.

Charitable Remainder Trust (CRT): A charitable trust that provides for a payment, at least annually, to at least one noncharitable income recipient for a period specified in the trust instrument, with the remainder of the income being paid to at least one charitable beneficiary. The objective of a charitable remainder trust is to shelter the donor's gift from estate taxes.

Common Area Expenses (CAM): Expenses that are common to all tenants leasing at a commercial real estate property. Typically, they are billed back to the tenants by the landlord.

Conduit CMBS loan: Commercial mortgage-backed securities (CMBS) are a type of security backed by commercial mortgages rather than residential real estate. CMBS are more complex and volatile than residential mortgage-backed securities due to the unique nature of the assets that secure the securities.

Contents insurance: Typically refers to coverage for property you own. With personal property protection, you're basically covering the personal possessions that you keep in your home. It can include everything from your laptop computer to your clothing. Typically, it covers the stuff that would fall out if you took your home or apartment and shook it.

Certified Property Manager (CPM): A real estate professional designation awarded by the Institute of Real Estate Management (IREM) and recognized by the National Association of Realtors (NAR).

Deductible: An insurance deductible is the amount of expenses that the insured must pay out of pocket before an insurer will pay any expenses. Depositor's forgery and alterations insurance: This protects your business from any losses resulting from forgery or alterations to checks, credit cards, promissory notes, or drafts that is drawn upon you or your accounts by people acting as your agent.

Depreciation (refers to two aspects of the same concept):
1. The decrease in value of assets, also known as fair value depreciation.
2. An imaginary savings holdback.
Residential properties are depreciated over 27.5 years; commercial 39 years; gas stations 15 years. For any other depreciation info, visit the IRS website.

Due diligence: Investigation a buyer completes in order to identify problems with a real estate investment. This includes investigation into the structure itself as well as the property and the financial records.

Errors and omissions: Refers to errors and omissions insurance, a specialized liability protection against losses not covered by traditional liability insurance. It protects you and your business from claims if you are sued for negligent acts, errors, or omissions committed during business activities that result in a financial loss for the client.

Escrow: A neutral third party to a contractual arrangement (attorneys or others that are licensed as escrow companies) in which the third party receives and disburses money and/or documents for the primary transacting parties; typically applies to real estate transactions.

Fidelity bond: Insurance protection that covers policyholders for losses that they incur as a result of fraudulent acts by specified individuals. It usually insures a business for losses caused by the dishonest acts of its employees. First trust deed: A legal document that gives your mortgage lender the right to foreclose and sell your property if you fall behind on your mortgage payments.

Force majeure clause (French for "superior force"): A contract provision that allows a party to suspend or terminate the performance of its obligations when certain circumstances (such as acts of God) beyond their control arise that make performance inadvisable, commercially impracticable, illegal, or impossible.

Guaranteed replacement cost coverage: An insurance policy that pays for the entire cost of replacing or repairing property, even if it is beyond the policy limit.

Hard money lender: Lending companies offering a specialized type of real-estate backed loan. They tend to lend short-term capital (also called bridge loans) that provide funding based on the value of real estate acting as collateral. Hard money lenders tend to focus on the value of the collateral property rather than the borrower's ability to repay the debt. They typically charge much higher interest rates than banks because they fund deals that do not conform to bank standards such as verification of borrower's income, assets, or credit score. Hard money lenders typically take a first trust deed position and are prepared to foreclose on the borrower if the borrower does not make his or her payments.

Liability insurance: A part of the insurance system that protects the insured from the risks of liabilities imposed by lawsuits and similar claims.

Lien: A right to keep possession of property belonging to another person until a debt owed by that person is discharged. Typically, a lien is recorded and of record.

Limited liability company (LLC): A business structure that combines the pass-through taxation of a partnership or sole proprietorship with the limited liability of a corporation. An LLC is not a corporation; it is a legal form of a company that provides limited liability to its owners in many jurisdictions.

Loss of rents coverage: Insurance that reimburses a landlord for lost income while the property is being repaired or rebuilt when the loss is covered by property insurance.

Market vacancy rate: While a vacancy rate is the ratio of rental units not rented versus the total number in the building, a market vacancy rate is the ratio of rental units not rented versus the total number in a specific defined marketplace.

NNN: See Triple Net Investments

Premium: The amount of money you pay to the insurance company to cover your insurance costs.

Property loss history: Insurance company loss history for a property. Insurance companies use this to decide how risky it is to insure a property.

Pull a permit: When you apply and then receive a permit from a city or county, typically for a construction of a building or a portion of a construction project. For example, one would pull a permit for water meters or a new water heater.

Rehabilitation loan: A loan pulled for rehabilitating a building.

Real Estate Investment Trust (REIT): Modeled after mutual funds, REITs invest only in real estate, such as office buildings; apartments; medical buildings; or retail buildings that provide investors of all types, stable income streams, diversification, and long-term capital appreciation. REITs typically pay out all of their taxable income as dividends to their shareholders. In turn, shareholders pay the income taxes on those dividends.

Renters insurance: A tenant insurance policy that will cover your property for damages caused by your tenant.

Rent-roll: A summary of rents in list format at an apartment or commercial property.

Reserve funds: Funds that are saved and held in reserve to offset future expenses. Often used for property tax, insurance, or property repairs.

Rider: A provision of an insurance policy that is purchased separately from the basic policy and provides additional benefits to the insured at additional cost.

Self-insure: When you reserve funds to pay for damages to a property. Typically, you reserve or underwrite risk and decide how much you want to pay out of pocket for damages and then buy insurance to cover the higher/more expensive risks.

Specifications worksheet: Specifications clearly developed for property repairs.

Tenant-in-common (TIC) investments: An investment by the taxpayer in real estate that is co-owned with other investors. Since the taxpayer holds the deed to real estate as a tenant in common, the investment qualifies under the like-kind rules of §1031. TIC investments are typically made in projects such as apartment houses, shopping centers, office buildings, etc. TIC sponsors arrange TIC syndications to comply with the limitations articulated by the IRS with Revenue

Procedure 2002-22 which, among other things, limits the number of investors to 35.

Triple-net (NNN) investments: Typically, single-tenant retail properties leased to tenants with high credit ratings on "net, net, net" terms (meaning the tenant is responsible for real estate taxes, insurance, and all maintenance). Typical lease terms range from 10–30 years. There are variations on the theme; for example, not all NNN investments cover all property ownership costs. Investors are cautioned to read leases very carefully.

Triple - Net expenses: Where the tenant agrees to pay all real estate taxes, insurance, utilities, interior maintenance and other lease defined expenses as part of their lease. Usually seen with retail and industrial tenancies, now being found in office leases as well.

Umbrella insurance: Liability insurance that is in excess of specified other policies and potentially primary insurance for losses not covered by the other policies.

Umbrella Partnership Real Estate Investment Trust (UPREIT): An UPREIT is an alternative to a section 1031 like-kind exchange as a way to defer or completely avoid capital gains tax liability when an individual or company wants to sell appreciated real estate. Instead of selling the property, the owner contributes it to an UPREIT in exchange for securities called "operating partnership units" or "limited partnership units." The partnership units are worth the same amount as the contributed property. Unlike selling the property, this transaction does not create a taxable event.

Upside value: Potential for gain in a real estate deal or transaction.

RESOURCES

Lennington Law Firm
"Should You Donate Real Estate to Charity?" http://lennington.com/global_pictures/Should you donate real estate to charity.pdf

Oregon Community Foundation
http://www.oregoncf.org/donors/give

Weikel Law Firm
"Should I Donate My House to Charity?"
http://www.weikellaw.com/news-story/should-i-donate-my-house-charity-part-4-donating-your-house-and-reserving-life-estate

ABOUT THE AUTHOR

Cliff Hockley is the president of Bluestone & Hockley Real Estate Services and the executive director of SVN | Bluestone & Hockley. He has been a licensed broker in both Washington and Oregon since 1986. He is a Certified Property Manager (CPM), and a Certified Commercial Investment Member (CCIM), which makes him one of very few highly trained professional real estate practitioners in the United States.

Cliff is experienced in all facets of property management and commercial brokerage and has managed and sold warehouse, office, and retail properties as well as mobile home parks, condominium associations, and residential properties of all sizes. Since 1986, he has helped build Bluestone & Hockley Real Estate Services into a company that manages over $2 billion worth of investments.

He has represented both buyers and sellers in the purchase and disposition of millions of dollars' worth of real estate transactions involving apartments, industrial complexes, and office buildings as well as Tenant in Common (TIC) investments. He has worked with financial institutions, governmental agencies, private investors, and not-for-profit organizations. He also has vast knowledge in budgeting, organizational management, and building structures.

Cliff holds an MBA from Willamette University's Atkinson Graduate School of Management (1981) and a BS in Political Science from Claremont McKenna College (1979). Among his many civic activities, Cliff served on the 2017 Portland, Oregon, Building Owner and Managers Association (BOMA) committee to revise the BOMA leases. He has served two stints on the Board of Directors for the Portland Chapter of the Institute of Real Estate Management (IREM), and in 2000 and 2003 he was recognized by IREM as Certified Property Manager of the Year, as well as Board Member of the Year in 2014. He has also served on the Board of the Rental Housing Alliance of Oregon, and in 2015 and 2016 he earned an achievement award in brokerage from SVN International.

He is a frequent contributor to industry publications, and his monthly newsletter "QuickFacts" has over 2,000 subscribers. He has also served as an adjunct professor in Real Estate at Portland State University (PSU) and helped draft the first property management curriculum for PSU.

9 781642 793208